Indiana

interactive SCIENCE

This red fox cub uses its tail for balance.

PEARSON

Glenview, Illinois • Boston, Massachusetts • Chandler, Arizona • Upper Saddle River, New Jersey

Authors

You are an author!

This is your own special book to keep. You can write all of your science discoveries in your book. That is why you are an author of this book.

Print your name, school, town, and state below. Then write to tell everyone all about you.

My Picture

Name

School

Town

State

All About Me

Credits appear on pages EM23–EM24, which constitute an extension of this copyright page.

ISBN-13: 978-0-328-52091-6
ISBN-10:   0-328-52091-8
2 3 4 5 6 7 8 9 10 V011 19 18 17 16 15 14 13 12 11

On The Cover
This red fox cub uses its tail for balance.

Program Authors

DON BUCKLEY, M.Sc.
Information and Communications Technology Director,
The School at Columbia University, New York, New York
Mr. Buckley has been at the forefront of K–12 educational technology for nearly two decades. A founder of New York City Independent School Technologists (NYCIST) and long-time chair of New York Association of Independent Schools' annual IT conference, he has taught students on two continents and created multimedia and Internet-based instructional systems for schools worldwide.

ZIPPORAH MILLER, M.A.Ed.
Associate Executive Director for Professional Programs and Conferences, National Science Teachers Association, Arlington, Virginia
Associate executive director for professional programs and conferences at NSTA, Ms. Zipporah Miller is a former K–12 science supervisor and STEM coordinator for the Prince George's County Public School District in Maryland. She is a science education consultant who has overseen curriculum development and staff training for more than 150 district science coordinators.

MICHAEL J. PADILLA, Ph.D.
Associate Dean and Director, Eugene P. Moore School of Education, Clemson University, Clemson, South Carolina
A former middle school teacher and a leader in middle school science education, Dr. Michael Padilla has served as president of the National Science Teachers Association and as a writer of the National Science Education Standards. He is professor of science education at Clemson University. As lead author of the *Science Explorer* series, Dr. Padilla has inspired the team in developing a program that promotes student inquiry and meets the needs of today's students.

KATHRYN THORNTON, Ph.D.
Professor and Associate Dean, School of Engineering and Applied Science, University of Virginia, Charlottesville, Virginia
Selected by NASA in May 1984, Dr. Kathryn Thornton is a veteran of four space flights. She has logged over 975 hours in space, including more than 21 hours of extravehicular activity. As an author on the *Scott Foresman Science* series, Dr. Thornton's enthusiasm for science has inspired teachers around the globe.

MICHAEL E. WYSESSION, Ph.D.
Associate Professor of Earth and Planetary Science, Washington University, St. Louis, Missouri
An author on more than 50 scientific publications, Dr. Wysession was awarded the prestigious Packard Foundation Fellowship and Presidential Faculty Fellowship for his research in geophysics. Dr. Wysession is an expert on Earth's inner structure and has mapped various regions of Earth using seismic tomography. He is known internationally for his work in geoscience education and outreach.

Understanding by Design® Author

GRANT WIGGINS, Ed.D.
President, Authentic Education, Hopewell, New Jersey
Dr. Wiggins is coauthor of *Understanding by Design®* (UbD), a philosophy of instructional design. UbD is a disciplined way of thinking about curriculum design, assessment, and instruction that moves teaching from content to understanding.

Planet Diary Author

JACK HANKIN
Science/Mathematics Teacher, The Hilldale School, Daly City, California Founder, Planet Diary Web site
Mr. Hankin is the creator and writer of Planet Diary, a science current events Web site. Mr. Hankin is passionate about bringing science news and environmental awareness into classrooms.

Activities Author

KAREN L. OSTLUND, Ph.D.
Advisory Council, Texas Natural Science Center, College of Natural Sciences, The University of Texas at Austin
Dr. Ostlund has more than 35 years of experience teaching at the elementary, middle school, and university levels. Previously Dr. Ostlund served as the Director of WINGS Online (Welcoming Interns and Novices with Guidance and Support) and the Director of the UTeach | Dell Center for New Teacher Success with the UTeach program in the College of Natural Sciences at the University of Texas at Austin. She also served as the Director of the Center for Science Education at the University of Texas at Arlington, President of the Council of Elementary Science International, and on the Board of Directors of the National Science Teachers Association. As an author of the *Scott Foresman Science* series, Dr. Ostlund was instrumental in developing inquiry activities.

ELL Consultant

JIM CUMMINS, Ph.D.
Professor and Canada Research Chair, Curriculum, Teaching and Learning Department at the University of Toronto
Dr. Cummins's research focuses on literacy development in multilingual schools and the role technology plays in learning across the curriculum. *Interactive Science* incorporates research-based principles for integrating language with the teaching of academic content based on Dr. Cummins's work.

Program Consultants

WILLIAM BROZO, Ph.D.

Professor of Literacy, Graduate School of Education, George Mason University, Fairfax, Virginia.
Dr. Brozo is the author of numerous articles and books on literacy development. He co-authors a column in The Reading Teacher and serves on the editorial review board of the Journal of Adolescent & Adult Literacy.

KRISTI ZENCHAK, M.S.

Biology Instructor, Oakton Community College, Des Plaines, Illinois
Kristi Zenchak helps elementary teachers incorporate science, technology, engineering, and math activities into the classroom. STEM activities that produce viable solutions to real-world problems not only motivate students but also prepare students for future STEM careers. Ms. Zenchak helps elementary teachers understand the basic science concepts, and provides STEM activities that are easy to implement in the classroom.

Content Reviewers

Paul Beale, Ph.D.
Department of Physics
University of Colorado
Boulder, Colorado

Joy Branlund, Ph.D.
Department of Earth Science
Southwestern Illinois College
Granite City, Illinois

Constance Brown, Ph.D
Atmospheric Science Program
Geography Department
Indiana University
Bloomington, Indiana

Dana Dudle, Ph.D.
Biology Department
DePauw University
Greencastle, Indiana

Rick Duhrkopf, Ph. D.
Department of Biology
Baylor University
Waco, Texas

Mark Henriksen, Ph.D.
Physics Department
University of Maryland
Baltimore, Maryland

Andrew Hirsch, Ph.D.
Department of Physics
Purdue University
W. Lafayette, Indiana

Linda L. Cronin Jones, Ph.D.
School of Teaching & Learning
University of Florida
Gainesville, Florida

T. Griffith Jones, Ph.D.
College of Education
University of Florida
Gainesville, Florida

Candace Lutzow-Felling, Ph.D.
Director of Education
State Arboretum of Virginia & Blandy Experimental Farm
Boyce VA 22620

Cortney V. Martin, Ph.D.
Virginia Polytechnic Institute
Blacksburg, Virginia

Sadredin Moosavi, Ph.D.
University of Massachusetts Dartmouth
Fairhaven, Massachusetts

Klaus Newmann, Ph.D.
Department of Geological Sciences
Ball State University
Muncie, Indiana

Scott M. Rochette, Ph.D.
Department of the Earth Sciences
SUNY College at Brockport
Brockport, New York

Karyn Rogers, Ph.D.
Department of Geological Sciences
University of Missouri
Columbia, Missouri

Laurence Rosenhein, Ph.D.
Dept. of Chemistry and Physics
Indiana State University
Terre Haute, Indiana

Sara Seager, Ph.D.
Department of Planetary Science and Physics
Massachusetts Institute of Technology
Cambridge, MA 02139

William H. Steinecker. Ph.D.
Research Scholar
Miami University
Oxford, Ohio

Paul R. Stoddard, Ph.D.
Department of Geology and Environmental Geosciences
Northern Illinois University
DeKalb, Illinois

Laurence Rosenhein, Ph. D.
Department of Chemistry
Indiana State University
Terre Haute, Indiana

Janet Vaglia, Ph. D.
Department of Biology
DePauw University
Greencastle, Indiana

Ed Zalisko, Ph.D.
Professor of Biology
Blackburn College
Carlinville, Illinois

1868
J.J. DANIELS, BUILDER

BRIDGETON

Built especially for
Indiana

Indiana *Interactive Science* covers 100% of Indiana's Academic Standards for Science without extraneous content. Built on feedback from Indiana educators, *Interactive Science* focuses on what is important to Indiana teachers and students, creating a personal, relevant, and engaging classroom experience.

Indiana K-8 Science Teacher Advisory Board

Jodi Allen
Glen Acres Elementary School
Lafayette, IN

Rick Dubbs
Monrovia Middle School
Monrovia, IN

Margaret Flack
Vincennes University
    Jasper Campus
Jasper, IN

Michael Gibson
New Haven Middle School
New Haven, IN

Jill Hatcher
Spring Mill Elementary School
Indianapolis, IN

Jamie Hooten
Lincoln Elementary School
Bedford, IN

Jamil Odom
Mary Bryan Elementary School
Indianapolis, IN

Mike Robards
Franklin Community Middle School
Franklin, IN

Richard Towle
Noblesville Middle School
Noblesville, IN

K-8 National Master Teacher Board

Tricia Burke
E. F. Young Elementary School
Chicago, IL

Lisa Catandella
Brentwood UFSD
Brentwood, NY

Karen Clements
Lynch Elementary School
Winchester, MA

Emily Compton
Park Forest Middle School
Baton Rouge, LA

Pansy Cowder
Lincoln Magnet School
Plant City, FL

Georgi Delgadillo
East Valley School District
Spokane, WA

Dr. Rick Fairman
McGregor School of Education
Antioch University
Yellow Springs, OH

Joe Fescatore
Green Elementary School
La Mesa, CA

Mimi Halferty
Gorzycki Middle School
Austin, TX

Christy Herring
Prairie Trace Elementary School
Carmel, IN

Treva Jeffries
Toledo Public Schools
Toledo, OH

James Kuhl
Central Square Middle School
Central Square, NY

Dr. Patsy Latin
Caddo Public School District
Shreveport, LA

Greg Londot
Hidden Hills Elementary School
Phoenix, AZ

Stan Melby
Sheridan Road Elementary
Fort Sill, OK

Bonnie Mizell
Howard Middle School
Orlando, FL

Dr. Joel Palmer
Mesquite ISD
Mesquite, TX

Leslie Pohley
Largo Middle School
Largo, FL

Susan Pritchard
Washington Middle School
La Habra, CA

Anne Rice
Woodland Middle School
Gurnee, IL

Adrienne Sawyer
Chesapeake Public Schools
Chesapeake, VA

Richard Towle
Noblesville Middle School
Noblesville, IN

Dr. Madhu Uppal
Schaumburg School District
Schaumburg, IL

Maria Valdez
Mark Twain Elementary School
Wheeling, IL

Viv Wayne
Montgomery County Public Schools
Rockville, MD

Indiana Unit A
Science, Engineering, and Technology

The Nature of Science

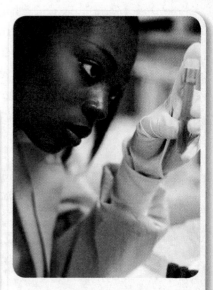

Scientists draw conclusions about the things they study.

mYscienceonLine.com

Untamed Science™
Watch the Ecogeeks as they learn about the nature of science.

Got it? 60-Second Video
Watch and learn about the nature of science.

Envision It!
See what you already know about the nature of science.

Science Songs
Sing about the nature of science.

I Will Know...
See how the key concepts about the nature of science come to life.

Technology and Tools

*Trains help many people
travel long distances.*

mYscienceonLine.com

UntamedScience
Ecogeeks answer your
questions about technology
and tools.

Got it? **60-Second Video**
Review lessons about
technology and tools in
60 seconds!

Science Songs
Listen to a catchy tune about
technology and tools!

MY PLANET DIARY
Discovery! Find out about
a new kind of train in My
Planet Diary.

Investigate It! Simulation
Investigate how a machine can
ring a bell in this online lab.

Indiana

Chapter

3

Indiana Unit B
Physical Science

Indiana Unit B
Physical Science 71

Matter

These bubbles in the picture are filled with gas.

myscienceonLine.com

Untamed Science
Ecogeeks answer your
questions about matter.

Got it? 60-Second Video
Review lessons about
matter in 60 seconds!

Envision It!
See what you already know
about matter.

Explore It! Animation
Watch this matter
experiment online!

Vocabulary Smart Cards
Mix and match matter
vocabulary.

Force and Motion

A kick will make a soccer ball move.

myscienceonline.com

Untamed Science™
Watch the Ecogeeks learn about force and motion.

Got it? 60-Second Video
Take one minute to learn about force and motion.

Envision It!
See what you already know about force and motion.

Science Songs
Listen to a catchy tune about force and motion.

Explore It! Animation
Quick and easy experiments about force and motion.

Indiana Unit C
Earth Science

Earth and Sky

Scientists measure weather to warn people about storms.

❶ **MY SCIENCE ONLINE.com**

Untamed Science™
Ecogeeks answer your
questions about Earth
and sky.

Got it? ⏱ 60-Second Video
Earth and sky lessons are
reviewed in a minute!

🌐 **MY PLANET DIARY**
Did you know? Learn about
where your drinking water
comes from.

Investigate It! Simulation
Explore your weather in this
online lab.

❓ **I Will Know...**
See what you've learned
about Earth and sky.

Life Cycles

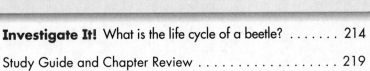

Some monarch butterflies begin their lives in Indiana.

myscienceonLine.com

Untamed Science
Watch the Ecogeeks learn about life cycles.

Got it? 60-Second Video
Take one minute to learn about life cycles.

Science Songs
Listen to a catchy tune about life cycles.

Explore It! Animation
Quick and easy experiments about life cycles.

I Will Know...
See how key concepts of each lesson about life cycles are brought to life!

"This is your book. You can write in it!"

interactive SCIENCE

Big Question

At the start of each chapter you will see two questions—an **Engaging Question** and a **Big Question.** Just like a scientist, you will predict an answer to the Engaging Question. Each Big Question will help you start thinking about Indiana's Big Ideas of science. Look for the symbol throughout the chapter!

Where does a cow get food?

136

Plants, Animals, and Their Habitats

Indiana
Chapter
5

Try It!	What does a cricket need?
Lesson 1	What do plants need to live? 1.3.3
Lesson 2	What do animals need to live? 1.3.5, 1.4.2
Lesson 3	How do plants and animals live in land habitats? 1.3.2, 1.3.4
Lesson 4	How do plants and animals live in water habitats? 1.3.2, 1.3.4
Lesson 5	What helps living things live in different places? 1.3.1
Investigate It!	Do plants need light?

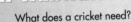

X on one thing a cow needs.

What do living things need?

Go to www.myscienceonline.com and click on:

 Untamed Science™
Ecogeeks answer your questions.

Got it? 60-Second Video
Review each lesson in 60 seconds!

137

Let's Read Science!

You will see a page like this toward the beginning of each chapter. It will show you how to use a reading skill that will help you understand what you read.

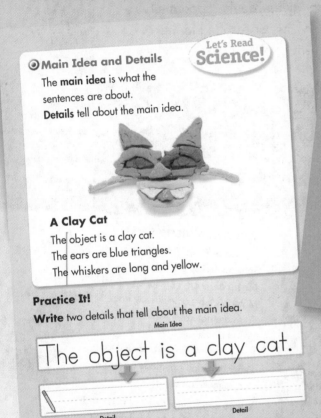

⊙ **Main Idea and Details**

The **main idea** is what the sentences are about.
Details tell about the main idea.

A Clay Cat
The object is a clay cat.
The ears are blue triangles.
The whiskers are long and yellow.

Practice It!
Write two details that tell about the main idea.

Main Idea

The object is a clay cat.

Detail   Detail

Let's Read Science!

75

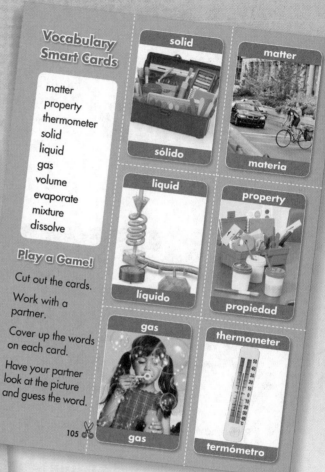

Vocabulary Smart Cards

matter
property
thermometer
solid
liquid
gas
volume
evaporate
mixture
dissolve

Play a Game!
Cut out the cards.
Work with a partner.
Cover up the words on each card.
Have your partner look at the picture and guess the word.

105 ✂

solid / sólido
matter / materia
liquid / líquido
property / propiedad
gas / gas
thermometer / termómetro

Vocabulary Smart Cards

Go to the end of the chapter and cut out your own set of **Vocabulary Smart Cards.** Draw a picture to learn the word. Play a game with a classmate to practice using the word!

mySCIENCEONLINE.com | Untamed Science

Look for **MyScienceOnline.com** technology options.
At MyScienceOnline.com you can immerse yourself in virtual environments, get extra practice, and even blog about current events in science.

"Engage with the page!"

interactive SCIENCE

Envision It!

At the beginning of each lesson, at the top of the page, you will see an **Envision It!** interactivity that gives you the opportunity to circle, draw, write, or respond to the Envision It! question.

Lesson 2

What are objects made of?

1.4.3 Use all senses as appropriate to sort objects as being composed of materials that are naturally-occurring or human-made, or a combination of the two. (Also 1.NS.5)

Envision It!

Tell three objects that people made.

UNLOCK
I will know how to sort objects by their materials.

Word to Know
natural

MY PLANET DIARY for Indiana

INVENTION!

Read Together

Do you like to eat popcorn? Orville Redenbacher wanted to invent corn that made the best popcorn. He tested many kinds of corn in Indiana. People test things to find what works best. People can test things they make. People can test things that grow on their own too.

Underline what Orville Redenbacher tested.

Write something you would like to test.

46

Different Materials

Objects are made of materials.
Some materials are natural.
Natural means not made by people.
Materials that come directly from Earth are natural.
Wood is natural.
Rocks and minerals are natural too.
Other materials are made by people.
People make plastic.

Write one natural material in the picture.

Write one material made by people.

47

MY PLANET DIARY

My Planet Diary interactivities will introduce you to amazing scientists, fun facts, and important discoveries in science. They will also help you to overcome common misconceptions about science concepts.

Read See DO!

After reading small chunks of information, stop to check your understanding. The visuals help teach about what you read. Answer questions, underline text, draw pictures, or label models.

Shape and Size

Shape is a property of matter. Matter can be different shapes such as round, flat, or square.

Size is a property of matter too. Matter can be big or small. Matter can be long or short.

You can use tools to measure the size of objects. You can use a ruler to measure small objects. You can use a meterstick to measure large objects.

Draw an X on two objects you would measure with a ruler.

Circle two objects you would measure with a meterstick.

Measure the length of the picture of the picnic blanket in centimeters.

_____ cm

Do the math! Count Rocks

Circle groups of ten rocks.
Count the tens.
Count the ones.
Add the number of rocks in the groups together.

1.
2.
3.

Do the math!

Scientists commonly use math as a tool to help them answer science questions. You can practice skills that you are learning in math class right in your Interactive Science Student Edition!

Got it?

At the end of each chapter you will have a chance to evaluate your own progress! At this point you can stop or go on to the next lesson.

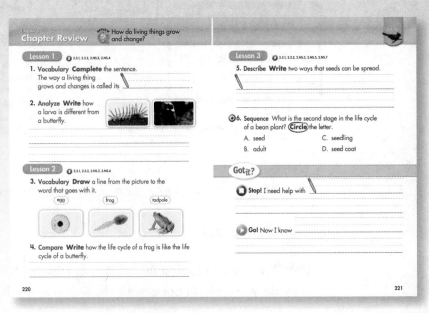

Chapter Review — How do living things grow and change?

Lesson 1

1. **Vocabulary Complete** the sentence. The way a living thing grows and changes is called its _____

2. **Analyze Write** how a larva is different from a butterfly.

Lesson 2

3. **Vocabulary Draw** a line from the picture to the word that goes with it.
egg   frog   tadpole

4. **Compare Write** how the life cycle of a frog is like the life cycle of a butterfly.

Lesson 3

5. **Describe Write** two ways that seeds can be spread.

6. **Sequence** What is the second stage in the life cycle of a bean plant? **Circle** the letter.
A. seed   C. seedling
B. adult   D. seed coat

Got it?

Stop! I need help with _____

Go! Now I know _____

220   221

"Have fun! Be a scientist!"

interactive SCIENCE

 Try It!

At the start of every chapter, you will have the chance to do a hands-on inquiry activity. The activity will provide you with experiences that will prepare you for the chapter lessons or may raise a new question in your mind.

Inquiry Try It!

How much force does it take to move objects?

A force is a push or a pull. Force can be measured.

Wear your safety goggles!

☐ **1.** Pick a material. Find a way to measure how much force it takes to move a book. Record.

☐ **2.** Measure the force needed to move 2 books. Record.

Explain Your Results

3. Explain how you measured force.

Materials

safety goggles   2 books

string

metric ruler

materials that stretch

Inquiry Skill
You measure when you compare the length of something to the ruler.

114

Lesson 3
What are magnets?

Envision It!

They are ___ ___ ___ ___ ___ ___.

Why do the letters stay on the refrigerator?

I will know that magnets can push or pull some metal objects.

Words to Know
attract
repel

 Inquiry Explore It!

What can a magnet pull through?

☐ **1.** Put a paper clip in a cup. Hold the magnet as shown.

☐ **2.** Record what you observe.

Can a magnet pull through these things?

	Plastic solid	Water liquid	Air gas	Paper solid
Yes				
No				

Explain Your Results

3. Interpret Data What can the magnet pull through?

Materials

magnet

paper clip   paper square

plastic cup   plastic cup with water

2.N5.2 Conduct investigations that may happen over time as a class, in small groups, or independently. (Also 2.1.4, 2.N5.1)

124

Magnets

Magnets can push or pull some metal objects.

Magnets attract some metal objects. **Attract** means to pull toward.

Magnets can repel other magnets. **Repel** means to push away.

The ability to attract and repel objects is a property of matter.

⊙ **Cause and Effect** Circle the objects that are attracted to the magnet. **Draw** an ✗ on the objects that are not attracted.

Tell why some of the objects were not attracted to the magnet.

125

 Explore It!

Before you start reading the lesson, **Explore It!** activities provide you with an opportunity to first explore the content!

xvi

STEM activities are found throughout core and ancillary materials.

Design It!

The **Design It!** activity has you use the engineering design process to find solutions to problems. By finding a problem and then planning, drawing, and choosing materials, you will make, test, and evaluate a solution for a real world problem. Communicate your evidence through drawings and prototypes and identify ways to make your solution better.

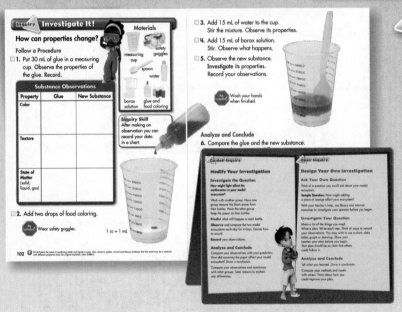

Investigate It!

At the end of every chapter, a Directed Inquiry activity gives you a chance to put together everything you've learned in the chapter. Using the activity card, apply design principles in the Guided version to Modify Your Investigation or the Open version to Develop Your Own Investigation. Whether you need a lot of support from your teacher or you're ready to explore on your own, there are fun hands-on activities that match your interests.

Apply It!

At the end of every unit, an Open Inquiry activity gives you a chance to explore science using scientific methods.

"Go online anytime!"

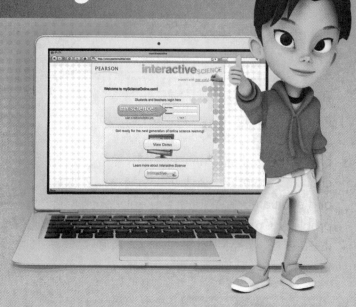

interactive SCIENCE

Here's how you log in...

1 Go to **www.myscienceonline.com**.

2 Log in with your username and password.

Username: _____

Password: _____

3 Click on your program and select your chapter.

Check it out!

Watch a Video!

UntamedScience™ Join the Ecogeeks on their video adventure.

Got it? 60-Second Video Review each lesson in 60 seconds.

Go Digital for Inquiry!

Explore It! Simulation Watch the lab online.

Investigate It! Virtual Lab Do the lab online.

Show What You Know!

Got it? Quiz Take a quick quiz and get instant feedback.

ISTEP+ Practice Prepare for the "big test."

Writing for Science Write to help you unlock the Big Question.

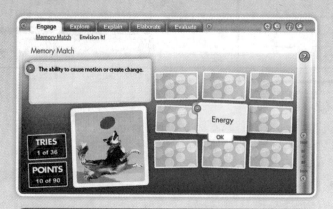

Get Excited About Science!

The Big Question Share what you think about the Big Question.

my planeT Diary Connect to the world of science.

Envision It! Connect to what you already know before you start each lesson.

Memory Match Play a game to build your vocabulary.

Get Help!

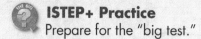 **my science COACH** Get help at your level.

Science, Engineering, and Technology

Chapter 1
The Nature of Science

What is science?

Chapter 2
Technology and Tools

How do people solve problems?

What does he want to ask?

The Nature of Science

Try It! What are the mystery objects?

Investigate It! What skills do scientists use?

Tell a partner what makes this boy a scientist.

 What is science?

Go to www.myscienceonline.com and click on: ✕

 UntamedScience™
Watch the Ecogeeks in this wild video.

 Got it? 60-Second Video
Review each lesson in 60 seconds!

What are the mystery objects?

Scientists listen to sounds to learn
new things.

Materials

6 mystery
boxes

☑ **1. Observe** Shake each box.
Listen to the sound.

Inquiry Skill
You can use what you
observe to **infer**.

☑ **2.** Look at the pictures. What could make each sound?

☑ **3. Infer** Write the letter of the box by each picture.

rice	tissue	5 noodles	paper clip	toothpick	2 metal marbles
C	E	F	B	D	A

☑ **4.** Open each box to find out what is inside.

Explain Your Results

5. Communicate Think like a scientist. Explain how you
decided what was in each box.

By lisnne atot thos
cups.

Picture Clues

Pictures can give you **clues** about what you read.

Scientists

Scientists use tools to investigate. This girl is a scientist. She measures. She observes. She observes some more. Soon she will learn something new!

Practice It!

Look at the picture. What are two tools that scientists use?

Scientists use tools.

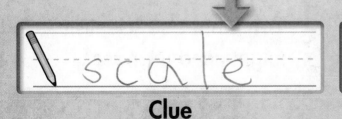

scale

Clue

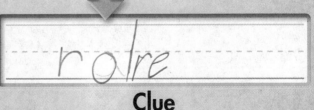

rolre

Clue

What questions do scientists ask?

2.NS.3 Generate questions and make observations about natural processes.

Envision It!

Tell one question scientists might ask about Mars.

MY PLANET DIARY

DISCOVERY

Read Together

Lunch is served! This astronaut put water back into her food. She is ready to eat!

Astronauts take food with them when they take off from the Kennedy Space Center in Florida. Scientists found a way to take food into space.

Many foods, like soup and macaroni and cheese, contain water. Scientists take water out of food so the food lasts longer. Astronauts put water back into the food before they eat it.

Tell what else scientists might need in space.

6

UNLOCK THE BIG ?

I will know that scientists ask questions and look for answers.

Word to Know

inquiry

Scientists

People who study the world around them are scientists. You are a scientist too. Scientists use inquiry to learn. **Inquiry** means asking questions and looking for answers.

This person asks questions about space. He uses a telescope to find answers.

This person is looking for answers to his questions about space.

⊙ **Picture Clues** How is the scientist learning about space? **Look** at the picture. **Write** what you see.

The scientist is learning about space.

He is using a telescope.

Clue

Clue

Scientists ask questions about plants.

Questions

Scientists ask questions about the world. Scientists ask questions about plants and animals. They ask questions about rocks and soil. They ask questions about space too. Scientists use inquiry to find answers to their questions.

Scientists know plants need soil to live and grow. They know there is no soil in space. They asked, "How might plants be grown in space without soil?" Then they looked for an answer.

Underline a question that scientists asked.

Write a question you might ask about plants in space.

How may grow

Discovery

Scientists discovered ways to grow plants without soil. They found out what nutrients plants need from soil. Then they added the nutrients to water. They put the roots of some plants in the water. They observed how the plants grew. Scientists shared what they learned. They explained how plants could grow in space without soil. Now they can grow plants in space.

(Circle) the discovery that scientists made.

Lightning Lab

Questions, Please
Write three questions that a scientist might ask about plants.

Draw an X to show where nutrients were added.

Scientists found an answer to their question. They are growing plants without soil.

These tomatoes were grown without soil.

9

What kinds of skills do scientists use?

Envision It!

2.NS.4 Make predictions based on observations.
2.NS.5 Discuss observations with peers and be able to support your conclusion with evidence.

Tell what you could learn about this market by using your senses.

Inquiry Explore It!

How can you sort objects?

Think about the skills you use as you do this activity.

Materials

paper shapes

☑ **1. Observe** Work alone. Think of one way to classify the shapes. Sort into groups.

_____

I classified the shapes by _____.

☑ **2.** Work with a group. Classify them in another way.

_____

We classified the shapes by _____.

Explain Your Results

3. Communicate What skills did you use to sort the shapes?

_____

_____

_____

2.DP.4 Select a solution to the need or problem.

Word to Know

observe

Different Ways to Learn

Scientists learn about the world around them. They find out what they know in many different ways. Scientists use their senses.

Scientists do experiments to learn. They do experiments again and again to make sure they get the same results.

These scientists want to know how tall the plant will grow.

Scientists learn from each other too. They ask each other, "How do you know?" They share what they learn. They give answers. They tell how they know.

Why might scientists want to learn from each other?

Science Skills

Observe

Scientists observe to find out about the world. You **observe** when you use your senses to find out about something.

How do you know when an apple is ripe? You might look at the color. Some people tap it to hear how it sounds. You might feel it and smell it too. You will know if it is ripe when you taste it!

Predict

Scientists use what they observe to predict. You predict when you tell what you think will happen.

How might scientists predict how many apples will grow? They may think about how many apples grew the year before.

⊙ **Picture Clues** How do you know this apple tree is healthy?

_____

_____

_____

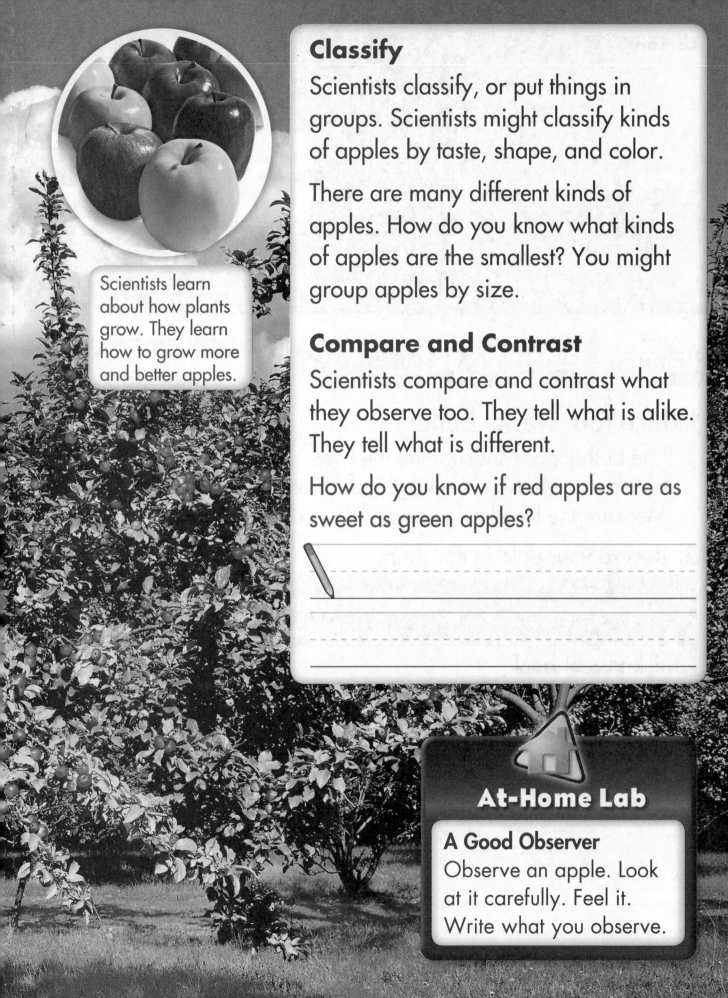

Scientists learn about how plants grow. They learn how to grow more and better apples.

Classify

Scientists classify, or put things in groups. Scientists might classify kinds of apples by taste, shape, and color.

There are many different kinds of apples. How do you know what kinds of apples are the smallest? You might group apples by size.

Compare and Contrast

Scientists compare and contrast what they observe too. They tell what is alike. They tell what is different.

How do you know if red apples are as sweet as green apples?

_____

_____

_____

At-Home Lab

A Good Observer
Observe an apple. Look at it carefully. Feel it. Write what you observe.

How do scientists use tools and stay safe?

2.NS.6 Make and use simple equipment and tools to gather data and extend the senses.

Envision It!

Tell one observation the beekeeper might make.

Inquiry **Explore It!**

Which tool works better?

☐ **1.** Use both tools. **Measure** the thickness of a book. Measure the height of a desk. Measure the length of your chalkboard.

☐ **2.** **Record** your data in the chart.

Materials

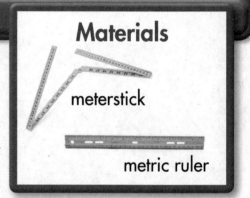

meterstick

metric ruler

	Measurement (cm)	Which tool worked better?
Thickness of book		
Height of desk		
Length of chalkboard		

Explain Your Results

3. Did the same tool always work better? Explain.

Word to Know

tool

Tools

Scientists use many different kinds of tools. A **tool** is something that is used to do work.

Some tools make objects look bigger. A hand lens helps a scientist observe a bee up close. Scientists use tools to stay safe too. A bee scientist wears a face cover and a body cover. The scientist wears gloves too.

Look at the picture of the bee. **Tell** what the bee's wings look like under the hand lens.

Use a hand lens to look at this picture. **Draw** what you see.

You can use a hand lens to study insects.

15

More Tools

You use many different kinds of tools to learn. Some tools are used to measure. Some tools help you stay safe. Read about the tools on these pages.

Circle two tools that are used to measure length.

A **thermometer** measures temperature. Most thermometers have a Celsius and a Fahrenheit scale. Most scientists use the Celsius scale.

You can use a **meterstick** to measure how long something is. Scientists use a meterstick to measure in centimeters.

You can use a **ruler** to measure how long something is too. Most scientists use a ruler to measure in centimeters or millimeters. You can use a ruler to measure in inches too.

You can use **safety goggles** to protect your eyes.

You can use a **magnet** to see if an object is made of certain metals.

Draw an X on the tool you would use to measure time.

A **stopwatch** or **timer** measures how long something takes.

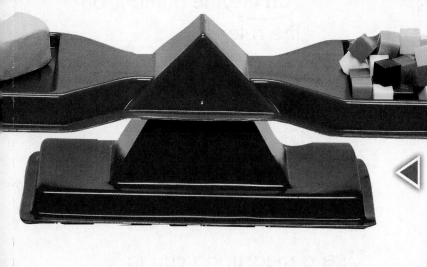

A **pan balance** is used to measure how much mass an object has. Objects that have a lot of mass feel heavy. Objects that do not have a lot of mass feel light.

You can use a **measuring cup** to measure volume. Volume is how much space something takes up.

Tell one way people might use a measuring cup at home.

Observe with Tools

Groups of scientists record the steps they take to answer questions. Another group of scientists may follow these steps. They should get the same answers if they follow the same steps and use the same tools.

Scientists compare what they observe with other scientists. Sometimes scientists get different answers. This might happen if a measuring tool is not used correctly. This might happen if the object being measured changes too. Scientists measure more than once to be sure their answers are correct.

Look at the picture. How long is the leaf? **Circle** the number on the ruler.

At-Home Lab

Measure Temperature
Use a thermometer to measure the outside temperature. Record the temperature in Fahrenheit and Celsius.

Use a measuring cup to measure two liquids.

_____ OZ

Compare your measurements with a partner's measurements.

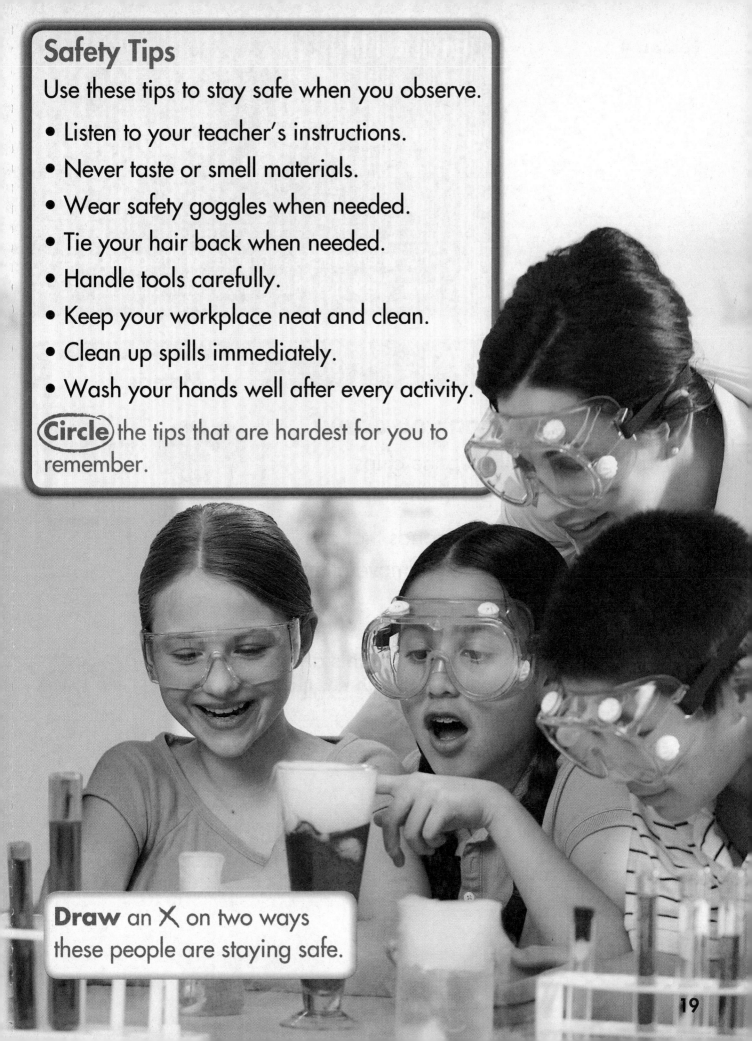

Safety Tips

Use these tips to stay safe when you observe.

- Listen to your teacher's instructions.
- Never taste or smell materials.
- Wear safety goggles when needed.
- Tie your hair back when needed.
- Handle tools carefully.
- Keep your workplace neat and clean.
- Clean up spills immediately.
- Wash your hands well after every activity.

Circle the tips that are hardest for you to remember.

Draw an X on two ways these people are staying safe.

19

How do scientists find answers?

Envision It!

2.NS.2 Conduct investigations that may happen over time as a class, in small groups, or independently. 2.NS.7 Recognize a fair test.

This scientist takes samples of the grass every year. **Tell** how the grass might change.

Inquiry Explore It!

What conclusion can you draw?

Materials

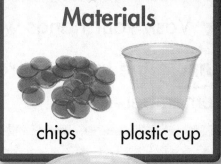

chips   plastic cup

☑ 1. Have a partner pick up the chips one at a time and put them in the cup.

☑ 2. Count the number of seconds that pass. **Record** how long it took to move all the chips.

Explain Your Results

3. Draw a Conclusion If you did this again, would you have the same result? Explain.

_____

_____

_____

_____

4. How could you improve your test?

_____

_____

_____

2.NS.2 Conduct investigations that may happen over time as a class, in small groups, or independently.
2.DP.4 Select a solution to the need or problem.

Words to Know

conclusion
hypothesis

Repeat Investigations

Scientists learn about the world around them. First they ask questions. Then they investigate. You investigate when you look for answers.

Scientists repeat investigations before they draw conclusions. A **conclusion** is what you decide after you think about all you know. You should be able to draw similar conclusions when you repeat an investigation.

For example, one scientist measures the height of the tallest tree in a forest. Others repeat the measurement. They get similar answers. They draw a conclusion.

Explain what would happen if other people repeat the same investigation as the scientist in the picture.

Scientists make conclusions from what they learn when they investigate.

21

Scientific Methods

Scientific methods are ways of finding answers. Some scientists use scientific methods when they do experiments. Scientific methods may have these steps. Sometimes scientists do the steps in a different order. Scientists do not always do all of the steps.

Ask a question.

Ask a question that you want answered.

Do seeds need water to grow?

Make your hypothesis.

A **hypothesis** is a possible answer to your question.

If seeds are watered, then they will grow because seeds need water.

Plan a fair test.

Change only one thing. Keep everything else the same. Record your steps. Someone else should get the same answer if they follow your steps.

Write the words *water* and *no water* to label the pots.

Use the same kinds of pots and soil. Water only one pot.

Do your test.

Test your hypothesis. Repeat your test. See if your results are the same.

Collect and record your data.

Keep records of what you observe. Use words, numbers, or drawings to help.

Go Green

Repeat a Test
Do plants need sunlight? Think of a hypothesis. Plan a test. Test your hypothesis. Record your steps. Repeat your test.

Tell your conclusion.

Think about the results of your test. Decide if your hypothesis is supported or not supported. Tell what you decide.

Seeds need water to grow.

Circle the question. **Underline** the hypothesis.

Explain what you think would happen if someone else followed the same steps in this investigation.

_____

_____

_____

How do scientists collect and share data?

Envision It!

2.NS.1 Use a scientific notebook to record predictions, questions and observations about data with pictures, numbers or in words.

Write what you observe about the rocks.

Inquiry **Explore It!**

What are different ways you can collect and share data?

How many boys and girls are in your class?

☑ **1.** Use the Tally Chart.

    Make 1 mark for each boy.

    Make 1 mark for each girl.

Tally Chart	
Boys	
Girls	

☑ **2.** Use the Picture Chart.

    Color 1 picture for each boy.

    Color 1 picture for each girl.

Picture Chart	
Boys	👤👤👤👤👤👤👤👤👤👤👤👤👤👤👤👤
Girls	👧👧👧👧👧👧👧👧👧👧👧👧👧👧👧

Explain Your Results

3. Communicate Share your charts with your family. Which did they like better?

_____

2.NS.2 Conduct investigations that may happen over time as a class, in small groups, or independently. (Also **2.NS.1**)

Word to Know

data

Collect Data

Scientists collect data to learn new things. **Data** is what you observe. You use your senses to collect data.

Scientists make conclusions from the data and from what they already know. Scientists infer when they make conclusions. You infer when you use what you know to explain something.

Underline what you use to observe data.

⊙ **Picture Clues Look** at the picture. What can you infer about the rocks?

25

Record Data

Scientists record what they observe and measure. They look at the data carefully.

Scientists can learn new things when they record data. Sometimes they find patterns. Sometimes they learn what is the same. Sometimes they learn what is different.

Look at the three rocks.
Measure how wide each rock is with a ruler.
Write the data in centimeters.

granite

basalt

pumice

At-Home Lab

Observe and Compare
Find three leaves in your neighborhood. Look at them carefully. Compare the shapes and colors. Measure them in inches.

26

Show Data

Scientists use charts and graphs to show data. A chart helps you organize data. A bar graph helps you compare data.

Use your data. **Fill in** this empty chart.

Comparing Rocks

	Width (centimeters)
Granite	
Basalt	
Pumice	

Use this empty bar graph. **Fill in** the bar for each rock.

Comparing Rocks

Width of Rock (centimeters)

9
8
7
6
5
4
3
2
1
0

Granite   Basalt   Pumice

Make a conclusion from your data.
Which rock is the widest?

_____

_____

What skills do scientists use?

Follow a Procedure

plain

salt

Materials

2 plastic cups with water

spoon

2 ice cubes

salt

timer

Inquiry Skill
You **interpret data** when you decide what the data means.

☑ **1.** Stir 1 spoonful of salt into the salt cup.

plain

salt

☑ **2.** Put 1 ice cube in each cup. Start the timer.

2.NS.2 Conduct investigations that may happen over time as a class, in small groups, or independently. **2.NS.3** Generate questions and make observations about natural processes. (Also **2.1.1, 2.NS.6**)

3. Check the timer when the first ice cube melts. **Record.**

4. Stop the timer when the second ice cube melts. Record.

Ice Cube Data	
	Time to Melt (minutes)
Plain water	
Salt water	

Analyze and Conclude

5. Interpret Data Did the ice cubes melt at the same rate? Explain.

_____

_____

_____

6. Name three science skills you used.

_____

_____

_____

Biography
Read Together

Shonte Wright

Shonte Wright knew she wanted to be a scientist and work at NASA when she was ten years old. She took many math and science classes to help her get ready for the job.

In 2003 NASA sent two robots to Mars. The robots were called rovers. Shonte Wright helped make sure the rovers would still work after the long trip through space.

Tell one question Shonte Wright might have asked about the rovers.

Rovers took pictures of Mars and sent them back to Earth. NASA used the pictures to study the planet.

Vocabulary Smart Cards

inquiry
observe
tool
conclusion
hypothesis
data

Play a Game!

Cut out the cards.

Work with a partner.

One person puts the cards picture side up.

The other person puts the cards picture side down.

Work together to match each word with its meaning.

conclusion

conclusión

inquiry

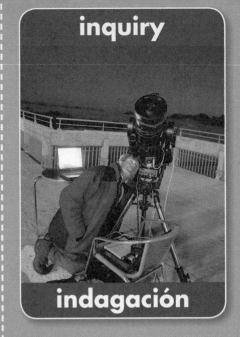

indagación

hypothesis

hipótesis

observe

observar

data

datos

tool

instrumento

asking questions and looking for answers

hacer preguntas y buscar respuestas

what you decide after you think about all you know

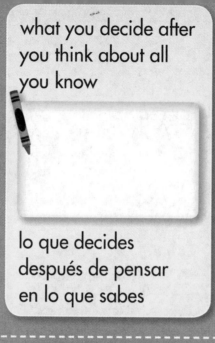

lo que decides después de pensar en lo que sabes

to use your senses to find out about something

usar tus sentidos para descubrir algo

a possible answer to a question

respuesta posible a una pregunta

something that is used to do work

algo que se usa para hacer trabajo

what you observe

lo que observas

 32

Lesson 1

What questions do scientists ask?

- Scientists use inquiry to learn about things.
- Scientists discover ways to solve problems.

Lesson 2

What kinds of skills do scientists use?

- Scientists observe and predict.
- Scientists classify and compare.

Lesson 3

How do scientists use tools and stay safe?

- Scientists use many different tools to learn.
- Hand lenses, rulers, and gloves are tools.

Lesson 4

How do scientists find answers?

- Scientists investigate and draw conclusions.
- A hypothesis is a possible answer to a question.

Lesson 5

How do scientists collect and share data?

- Scientists use their senses to collect data.
- Scientists show data in charts and bar graphs.

Lesson 1
2.NS.3

1. **⦿Picture Clues** The girl in the picture is using inquiry to learn about plants. What is she learning about the plant?

_____

2. **Apply** Some scientists ask questions about space. **Write** a question you have about space.

_____

_____

_____

Lesson 2
2.NS.4, 2.NS.5

3. **Vocabulary Complete** the sentence.

You _____ when you use your senses to find out about something.

4. **Describe Look** at the picture. **Write** something you observe about this rock.

_____

_____

_____

Lesson 3 ● 2.NS.6

5. Classify What is a tool that can help you stay safe?
(Circle) the letter.

A. meterstick   C. goggles

B. stopwatch   D. magnet

Lesson 4 ● 2.NS.2, 2.NS.7

6. Evaluate Why might a scientist repeat investigations?

_____

_____

_____

Lesson 5 ● 2.NS.1

7. Analyze Look at the picture.
What can you infer about this plant?

_____

_____

Got it?

☐ **Stop!** I need help with _____

▶ **Go!** Now I know _____

How do computers help you?

Technology and Tools

Try It! How can you keep an ice cube from melting?

Lesson 1 What is technology?
2.4.2, 2.NS.4

Lesson 2 How do people design new things?
2.4.3, 2.NS.6, 2.DP.1, 2.DP.4, 2.DP.5, 2.DP.9

Lesson 3 How do we use tools and machines?
2.4.1, 2.4.3

Investigate It! How can a machine ring a bell?

Tell how you use a computer.
Tell about another kind of technology that is important to you.

How do people solve problems?

Go to www.myscienceonline.com and click on:

 UntamedScience™
Ecogeeks answer your questions.

Got it? 60-Second Video
Take one minute to learn science!

Envision It!
See what you already know about science.

 **Science Songs**
Sing along with animated science songs!

How can you keep an ice cube from melting?

☑ **1.** Put an ice cube in each of 2 cups.

☑ **2.** **Design** a way to keep one cube from melting. Make and test your design.

☑ **3.** Wait 10 minutes. **Observe.** Compare the 2 ice cubes.

Materials

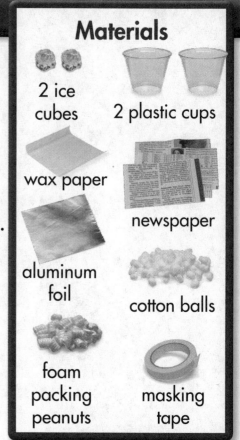

2 ice cubes

2 plastic cups

wax paper

newspaper

aluminum foil

cotton balls

foam packing peanuts

masking tape

Explain Your Results

4. Communicate

Draw and label your **design.**

Inquiry Skill
You **communicate** when you draw and label diagrams.

ⓘ **2.DP.1** Identify a need or problem to be solved. **2.DP.8** Communicate the solution with drawings or prototypes. (Also **2.DP.5**)

Main Idea and Details

The **main idea** is the most important idea in what you are reading. **Details** tell about the main idea.

Telephones

Telephones have changed. Long ago, most telephones were attached to a wall by wires. Today you can carry a telephone with you. Telephones are much smaller and lighter today than they were years ago.

Practice It!

Write two details about how telephones have changed.

Telephones have changed over the years.

Main Idea

Detail

Detail

39

What is technology?

Envision It!

2.4.2 Identify technologies developed by humans to meet a human need and investigate the limitations of the technology and how it has improved quality of life. (Also 2.NS.4)

Tell what problem the train helps solve.

my planet Diary

INVENTION!

Read Together

Engineers have designed a train that uses magnets instead of engines. These trains are called Maglev trains. They are faster and quieter than trains that use engines. Maglev trains float about one to ten centimeters above a guideway. The magnets on the bottoms of the trains and the magnets on the guideway help move the train along. Maglev trains can travel faster than 300 miles per hour!

Use a ruler. **Draw** a line that is ten centimeters tall to show how high Maglev trains can float.

guideway

Words to Know

technology

invent

Technology

People ride in cars. People use computers. We can do these things because of technology. **Technology** is the use of science to solve problems.

Sometimes people use technology to invent things. **Invent** means to make something for the first time.

Technology has made many things easier for people. Cars and trains are technology. They help people travel long distances. However, technology does not solve every problem. Cars and trains can break and stop working.

Tell one way computers help people. **Tell** one problem computers do not solve.

Scientists make cars that use electricity. These cars help reduce pollution.

41

Lightning Lab

A New Way
Think about a pencil. How do you think people wrote before pencils and pens were invented? Tell how you think people will write in the future.

Solve Problems

Engineers are people who design new things. They look for better ways to solve problems. They use science and technology to invent and discover new things.

Some people have trouble seeing. People used technology to solve this problem. People invented glasses. Glasses help people see better. Glasses are technology.

◉ **Main Idea and Details** **Underline** a problem that technology solves.

Read about technology below. **Pick** one technology. **Tell** what kind of problem it solves.

Technology Over Time

1879
The light bulb is mass-produced.

1885
A car that uses gasoline is invented.

1903
The Wright brothers fly their plane in Kitty Hawk, North Carolina.

1946
The first microwave oven is built.

Help People

Technology can help people stay healthy too. Doctors use technology to find out why people are sick.

People invented X rays. X rays are tools doctors can use to see inside people. Doctors can help people to get well after they find out what is wrong.

Draw another kind of technology. **Tell** what problem it solves. **Tell** one problem it does not solve.

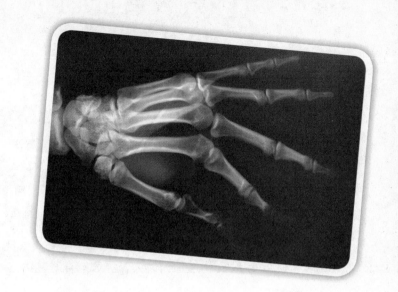

1975
The digital camera is invented.

2008
Text messaging is popular.

Draw something you would like to invent.

Lesson 2

How do people design new things?

Envision It!

2.4.3 Identify a need and design a simple tool to meet that need. **2.DP.1** Identify a need or problem to be solved. **2.DP.9** Communicate how to improve the solution. (Also **2.NS.6**, **2.DP.4**, **2.DP.5**)

Tell what you might like to design.

Inquiry **Explore It!**

How can you keep warm water warm?

☑ **1.** Fill 2 cups with warm water. **Measure** both temperatures. **Record.**

☑ **2.** **Cover** one with foil, plastic, or a paper towel.

☑ **3.** Wait 10 minutes. Measure. Record.

Materials

warm water

plastic wrap

tape

paper towel

foil

2 cups   thermometer

Explain Your Results

4. Infer How did you keep the water warm?

Temperature Chart

Cup of water	Starting (°C)	After 10 min (°C)
Not covered		
Covered		

2.DP.4 Select a solution to the need or problem. **2.DP.5** Select the materials to develop a solution. **2.DP.7** Evaluate and test how well the solution meets the goal.

Words to Know

goal
material

A Problem and a Goal

Engineers think about a problem that needs to be solved. Then they set a goal to find a solution to the problem. A **goal** is something you want to do.

Chester Greenwood lived a long time ago in Maine. Chester had a problem. His ears got very cold in the winter. He set a goal. He wanted to find a way to keep his ears warm.

Think about a problem you want to solve. **Write** your goal.

Maine can get very cold in the winter.

45

Plan and Draw

Engineers plan and draw before they make new things. Sometimes they plan and draw more than once.

Chester Greenwood planned to use a heavy wool scarf to stay warm. He tied it around his head. It kept his ears warm. However, the wool scarf was very itchy.

Chester wanted to find a better solution to his problem. Chester planned again. He planned to make earflaps to cover his ears.

Look at the drawings to see what Chester's plan might have looked like.

  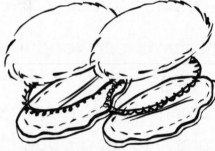

1. Make wire loops.   2. Cover loops.   3. Sew covers around wire loops.

Think of a problem. **Draw** something that would solve the problem. **Tell** how it solves your problem.

Choose Materials

Engineers choose materials to make new things. A **material** is what something is made of. Materials can be very different. Some materials are soft. Other materials are hard. Some materials are light. Other materials are heavy.

(Circle) materials you would want to use to keep your ears warm. **Tell** why.

At-Home Lab

Different Designs
Find out about two kinds of shoes. What are the shoes used for? Tell how the designs are different.

cotton

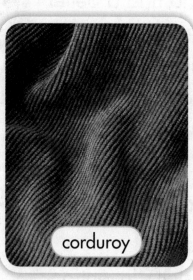

corduroy

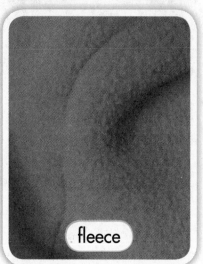

fleece

rubber

Draw a different material you might want to use. **Tell** about your drawing.

47

Make and Test

Engineers make and test the solution to their problem. They want to find out how well their design works. Sometimes they change their design. They do this to make their design better.

Chester made oval loops out of wire. Then he covered the loops with soft materials. Chester's earflaps kept his ears warm.

However, Chester wanted to find a better way to keep the earflaps in place. He changed his design. He made his design better by adding a flat steel spring to fit over his head. This kept the earflaps in place over his ears.

Underline why Chester changed his design.

How could you make Chester's invention even better?

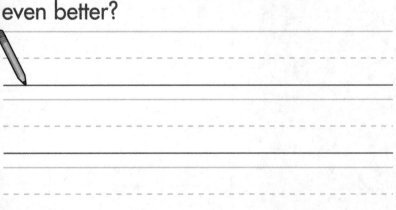

Record and Share

Engineers record what they have done. They write about their designs. They draw and label their designs too. Recording helps them remember what they have done. Sometimes engineers share what they have done with others.

Write headband or earflap to label the parts of these earmuffs.

This girl is wearing earmuffs. There are many different kinds of earmuffs today.

How do we use tools and machines?

2.4.1 Identify parts of the human body as tools, such as hands for grasping and teeth for cutting and chewing. 2.4.3 Identify a need and design a simple tool to meet that need.

Envision It!

Tell what kinds of tools you think were used to build this tree house.

Inquiry Explore It!

How does a lever work?

☐ **1.** Set up the ruler, pencil, and book as shown.

☑ **2.** Push down on the end of the lever. **Observe.**

☑ **3.** Repeat with the pencil at 15 cm and at 10 cm.

Explain Your Results

4. When was it easiest to lift the book?

_____

_____

5. Name two things people use that are levers.

_____

_____

Materials

wooden ruler

book

pencil

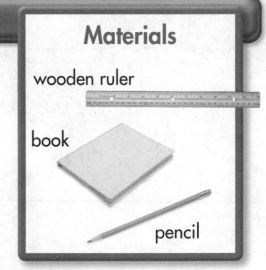

5 cm   20 cm

lever

UNLOCK THE BIG ? I will know about tools and simple machines. I will know how some body parts can be used as tools.

Words to Know

simple machine

Tools and Machines

Suppose you want to move an object. You might use a tool to help you. A machine is a tool that can make work easier. Sometimes tools and machines can do things that your body cannot do on its own.

A **simple machine** is a tool with few or no moving parts. A screw is a simple machine. A screw is used to hold things together.

A wagon is a machine. You can use a wagon to move heavy things. You can use a wagon to move many things at one time.

Draw one object that is held together by screws.

51

Simple Machines

There are many different kinds of tools and machines. Levers and wedges are simple machines. Pulleys and inclined planes are simple machines too.

pulley

Pulleys move an object up, down, or sideways. An inclined plane is flat. It is higher at one end than at the other. An inclined plane makes it easier to move things.

Look at the picture below. **Circle** the part that is the inclined plane.

Tell how the pulley moves the flag.

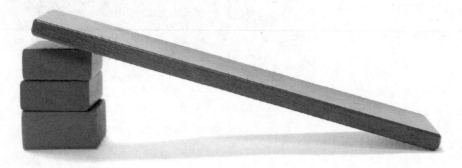

Suppose you need to move a heavy box. What could you use to help you move it? **Design** a tool to help you.

Body Parts as Tools

Think about different parts of your body. You can use some parts of your body as tools. You can use your body to do work.

shovel

A lever is a tool. A lever can be used to move things. A shovel is a lever. It can move dirt. You can use your arms as levers. You can use your arms to pick things up.

arms

tongs

These tongs are made of two levers. Levers can be used to grasp objects. You can use your hands as levers. You can use your hands to grasp a ball.

hands

knife

A wedge is a tool. A wedge is used to push things apart. A knife is a wedge. You can use your teeth as a wedge. You can use your teeth to cut and chew food.

teeth

Underline two simple machines on this page.

What other body part can you use as a tool? **Explain.**

Animal Body Parts as Tools

Think about different animals. Animals use body parts as tools. Gophers use their claws to dig into the ground. Woodpeckers use their beaks to drill into trees. Animals use their body parts to do work.

Tell what body parts a dog might use as a tool.

The beaver has long front teeth. It uses its teeth as a wedge to cut into wood.

teeth

wedge

The blue jay uses its beak to hold on to food. Its beak is like two levers.

levers

beak

Draw another animal that can use body parts as tools.
Tell about the animal you drew.

The sea turtle uses its hind flippers as shovels, or levers. It kicks sand out of the way to build a nest.

lever

flippers

Badger claws are like wedges. The claws help the badger dig into the ground.

wedge

claws

55

How can a machine ring a bell?

Follow a Procedure

☑ **1. Design** a way to ring a bell from one meter away. Use two simple machines.

☑ **2.** Draw your plan.

Materials

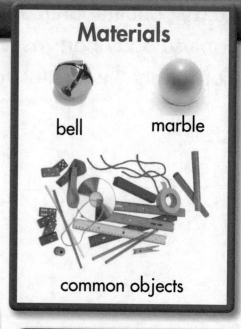

bell   marble

common objects

Inquiry Skill
You **infer** when you get ideas from what you learn.

2.DP.2 Brainstorm potential solutions. **2.DP.3** Document the design throughout the entire design process. **2.DP.6** Create the solution. (Also **2.DP.9**)

☐ **3. Record** what materials you will use.

_____

_____

_____

☐ **4.** Test your design.
My machine (**did / did not**) ring the bell.

☐ **5.** Evaluate your design. How could you **redesign** your machine to ring the bell better?

_____

_____

_____

Analyze and Conclude

6. Communicate   What simple machines did you use?

_____

_____

_____

7.   **Infer**   How do simple machines help people?

_____

_____

_____

Studebaker
National Museum

You can visit the Studebaker National Museum in South Bend. The Studebaker company started in 1868. At first the company made wagons. As time passed, technology changed. Studebaker began making automobiles. Some of their cars were powered by gasoline. Some of their cars were powered by electricity. Studebaker produced cars until 1966.

Write how technology affected the Studebaker company.

Vocabulary Smart Cards

technology
invent
goal
material
simple
machine

Play a Game!

Cut out the cards.

Work with a group.

Tape a card to the back of each group member.

Give each person clues about his or her word.

Have everyone guess his or her word.

material

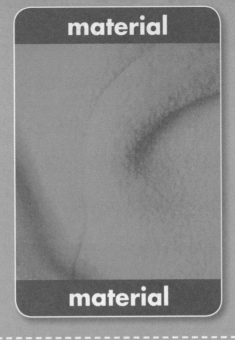

material

technology

tecnología

simple machine

máquina simple

invent

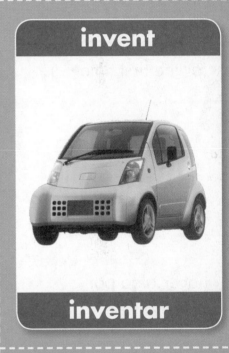

inventar

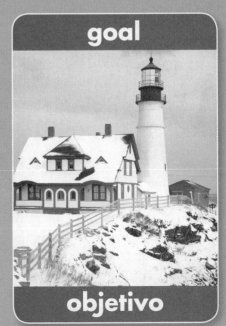

objetivo

goal

the use of science to
solve problems

el uso de la ciencia
para resolver
problemas

what something is
made of

de lo que está hecho
algo

to make something
for the first time

hacer algo por
primera vez

tool with few or no
moving parts

instrumento sin, o con
pocas, partes que se
mueven

something you want
to do

algo que quieres
hacer

Lesson 1 What is technology?

- Technology is the use of science to solve problems.
- Invent means to make something for the first time.

Lesson 2 How do people design new things?

- People set a goal, plan, draw, choose materials, make, test, record, and share.

Lesson 3 How do we use tools and machines?

- Simple machines can make work easier.
- You can use some parts of your body as tools.

Chapter Review

How do people solve problems?

Lesson 1 2.4.2, 2.NS.4

1. **Describe Think** about one kind of technology you use. **Write** how it helps you.

2. **Main Idea and Details Read** the paragraph below. **Underline** two details.

   Technology has changed the way people have fun. People listen to music on MP3 players. People use computers to play games.

Lesson 2 2.4.3, 2.NS.6, 2.DP.1, 2.DP.4, 2.DP.5, 2.DP.9

3. **Vocabulary Complete** the sentence. **Circle** the letter. Chester Greenwood wanted to find a way to keep his ears warm. He set a _____.

   A. problem   C. goal

   B. record   D. test

4. **Evaluate Circle** the earmuffs that you would want to wear. **Tell** why.

5. Classify Draw a line from the picture to the term that goes with it.

pulley screw inclined plane

6. Describe Write one way you can use your hands as tools.

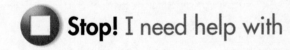

_____

_____

_____

Got it?

□ **Stop!** I need help with _____

_____

_____

▶ **Go!** Now I know _____

_____

_____

How would you design a pencil?

The earliest versions of pencils were made by adults.
They made the pencils for adults to use. **Design** a pencil.

Find a problem.

☑ **1.** List 3 things you would change about a pencil.
Tell why you would make each change.

Change A: _____

_____

Change B: _____

_____

Change C: _____

_____

Plan and draw.

☑ **2.** Pick one thing to change. Make a step-by-step plan.
You will use the materials from the next page.
Tell how you would test your **design.**

☑ **3.** Draw your design. Label each material.

2.4.2 Identify technologies developed by humans to meet a human need and investigate the limitations of the technology and how it has improved quality of life. **2.4.3** Identify a need and design a simple tool to meet that need. **2.DP.1** Identify a need or problem to be solved. **2.DP.2** Brainstorm potential solutions. **2.DP.3** Document the design throughout the entire design process. **2.DP.4** Select a solution to the need or problem. **2.DP.5** Select the materials to develop a solution. **2.DP.6** Create the solution. **2.DP.7** Evaluate and test how well the solution meets the goal. **2.DP.8** Communicate the solution with drawings or prototypes. **2.DP.9** Communicate how to improve the solution.

Choose materials.

☑ **4.** Circle the materials you will use.

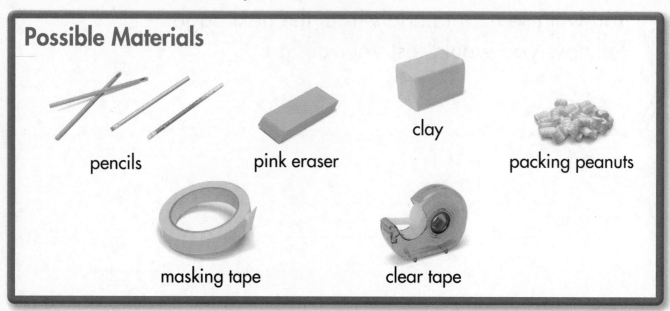

Possible Materials

pencils

pink eraser

clay

packing peanuts

masking tape

clear tape

☑ **5.** Tell how you will use each material.

Make and test.

☐ **6.** Make the new pencil you **designed.** Follow your plan.

☐ **7.** Test your pencil design by filling in the chart below.
Use a regular pencil. Then use the pencil you designed.

Pencil Chart		
	Regular Pencil	**Pencil You Designed**
Print Pencil. Pencil		
Handwrite Pencil. *Pencil*		
Print 3 + 5 = 8. $3 + 5 = 8$		
Draw the hammer. 		

Record and share.

☑ **8.** Use your new pencil for one day.
Record when you used your pencil.
Record your **observations** about how well it worked.

9. What about your pencil **design** worked well?

10. What about your pencil design did not work well?

11. How could you **redesign** your pencil?

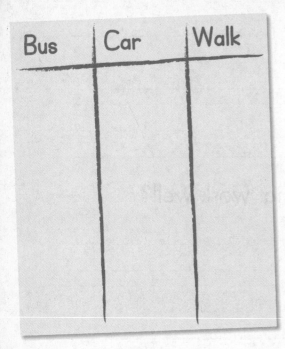

Bus	Car	Walk

Using Scientific Methods

1. Ask a question.
2. Make a hypothesis.
3. Plan a fair test.
4. Do your test.
5. Collect and record data.
6. Tell your conclusion.

Travel to School

- Do more classmates come to school on a bus, in a car, or by walking?
- Make a hypothesis.
- Use a chart and collect data.

2.NS.1, 2.NS.5

Design a Solution

- Think of a problem you want to solve.
- Plan and draw your solution in a notebook.
- Label your drawing.
- List the materials you would use.
- Share your design with a partner.

2.4.3, 2.DP.1, 2.DP.4, 2.DP.5, 2.DP.8

Write a Song

- Write a song about technology.
- Give your song a name and sing it to the class.

2.4.2

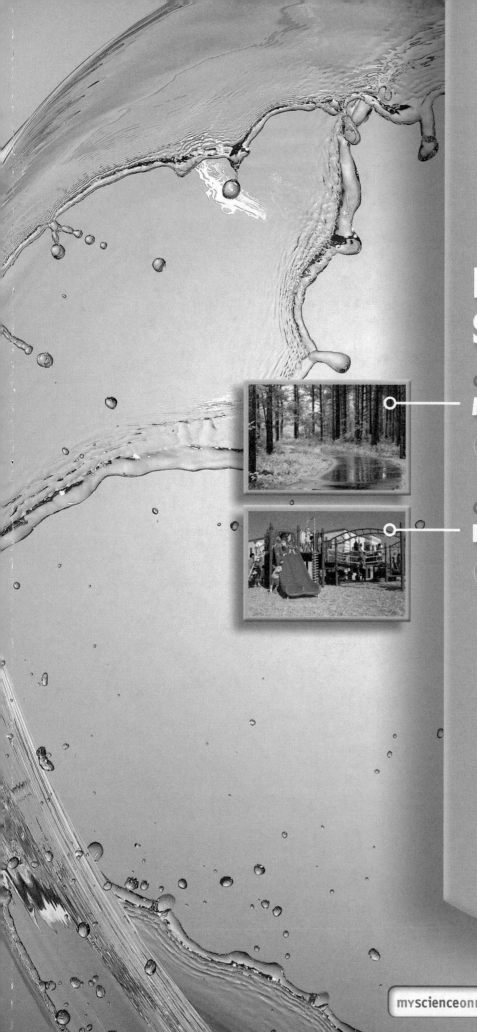

Physical Science

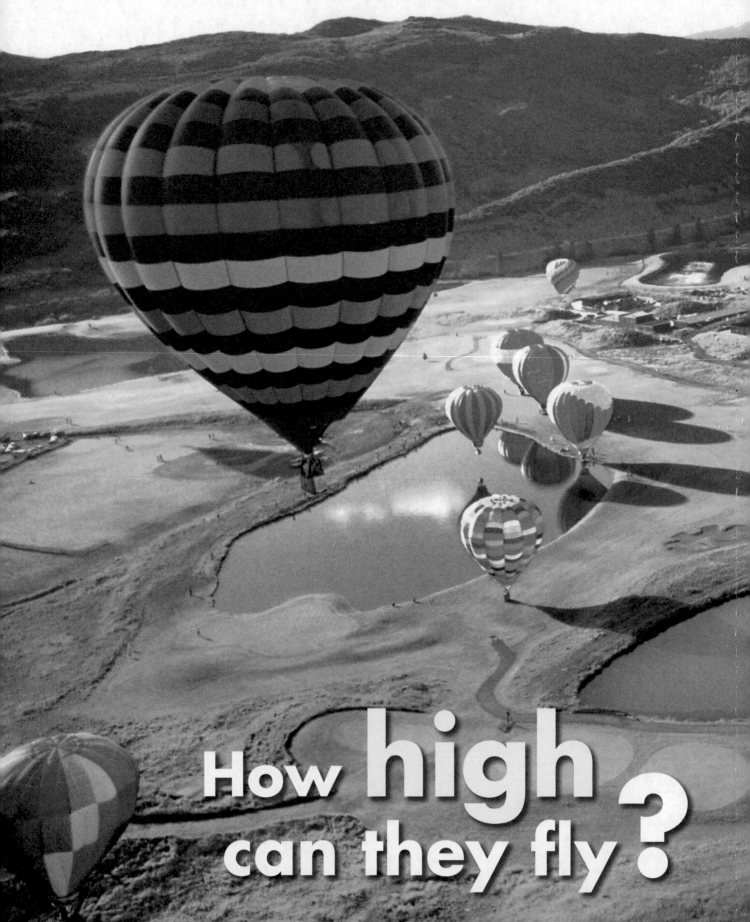

How high can they fly?

Matter

 Try It! **What affects evaporation?**

Lesson 1 What are some properties of matter?
2.1.1, 2.NS.3, 2.NS.4, 2.NS.5, 2.NS.6

Lesson 2 What are solids, liquids, and gases?
2.1.1, 2.NS.2, 2.NS.3

Lesson 3 How can water change?
2.1.1, 2.NS.2, 2.NS.3

Lesson 4 What are mixtures?
2.1.2, 2.1.3, 2.NS.2, 2.NS.3, 2.NS.4

 Investigate It! **How can properties change?**

Tell what you think makes these balloons fly.

How does matter change?

Go to www.myscienceonline.com and click on:

Untamed Science
Ecogeeks answer your questions.

Got it? 60-Second Video
Take one minute to learn science!

Envision It!
See what you already know about science.

Science Songs
Sing along with animated science songs!

73

What affects evaporation?

Evaporation is changing a liquid to a gas.

Materials

2 plastic cups half full of water

marker

1 lid

☐ **1.** Put a lid on one cup.

☐ **2.** Draw a line to show the water level.

☐ **3.** **Collect Data** Each day draw a line to show the water level.

Inquiry Skill You **collect data** when you record what you observe.

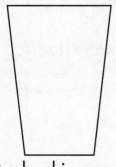

water level in open cup

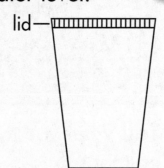

water level in covered cup

Explain Your Results

4. Communicate What happened to the water level in each cup?

_____

_____

_____

5. Explain any differences in group results.

_____

_____

_____

_____

2.1.1 Observe, describe, and measure ways in which the properties of a sample of water (including volume) change or stay the same as it is heated and cooled and is transformed into different states. (Also **2.NS.2**)

◉ Draw Conclusions

You **draw conclusions** when you decide about something you see or read.

A Hot Day

You are playing outside on a hot day. You bring a glass of ice water with you to drink. After a while, you notice that the ice is gone.

Practice It!

Write what you think happened to the ice.

I know	My conclusion
It is a hot day. →	

What are some properties of matter?

2.1.1 Observe, describe, and measure ways in which the properties of a sample of water (including volume) change or stay the same as it is heated and cooled and is transformed into different states. (Also 2.NS.3, 2.NS.4, 2.NS.5, 2.NS.6)

Envision It!

Circle the orange that sank.

mY pLaneT DiaRY

Fact or Fiction?

Read Together

Have you ever seen icicles on oranges? Oranges grow in warm places. It almost never gets cold enough for icicles. Icicles do not stay around long when they do form. What happens to them?

Icicles seem to disappear when they melt and become puddles of water. After a while, the puddles seem to disappear too!

What do you think happens to puddles?

_____

_____

_____

_____

Draw one object that you think will float.

UNLOCK THE BIG ?

I will know that matter has many different properties.

Words to Know

matter
property
thermometer

Matter

Everything you see around you is made of matter. **Matter** is anything that takes up space and has mass. Mass is the amount of matter in an object. Objects that have a lot of matter are heavy. The car in the picture is heavy. Objects that do not have a lot of matter are light. The bicycle is light.

Some things you cannot see are made of matter. The air around you has matter.

The cars and the bike are made of matter.

◎ **Draw Conclusions Write** a conclusion about the mass of a car.

I know

A car has a lot of matter.

My conclusion

_____
_____
_____

77

Properties of Matter

Different kinds of matter have different properties. A **property** is something about an object that you can observe with your senses. You can describe matter by telling about its properties. Weight is a property of matter. Weight is how heavy or light something is.

Find an object in your classroom.
Tell its color.
Measure its weight. **Use** a scale.

The tape is sticky.

At-Home Lab

Magnets
Gather some objects. Get a magnet. Tell which objects the magnet pulls. Tell which objects the magnet does not pull.

Color and Texture

Color is a property of matter. Matter can be brown, purple, blue, or any other color you can think of.

Texture is a property of matter. Texture is how something feels. Objects can feel smooth or rough. The top of a table is smooth. A dry sponge is rough.

Find a yellow object in the picture. **Tell** about its texture.

These pipe cleaners are red, yellow, and green.

Shape and Size

Shape is a property of matter. Matter can be different shapes such as round, flat, or square.

Size is a property of matter too. Matter can be big or small. Matter can be long or short.

You can use tools to measure the size of objects. You can use a ruler to measure small objects. You can use a meterstick to measure large objects.

Draw an ✗ on two objects you would measure with a ruler.

ruler

Circle two objects you would measure with a meterstick.

meterstick

Measure the length of the picture of the picnic blanket in centimeters.

_____

_____ cm

Sink or Float

Whether an object sinks or floats is a property of matter.

The golf ball sinks to the bottom of the vase. The table-tennis ball floats at the top of the vase.

Look at the picture of the vase. **Draw** another object that you think will sink.

Circle the object below that you think will float.

Temperature

Temperature is a property of matter. It tells how hot or cold something is.

A **thermometer** is a tool that measures temperature. A thermometer can measure the temperature of the air. The red liquid in the thermometer below goes up when it is getting warmer. The red liquid goes down when it is getting colder. The number next to the top of the red liquid is the temperature.

Fill in the thermometer below to show how 5° Celsius (41°F) would look.

Write the difference in temperature between the two thermometers.

This thermometer shows that it is 30° Celsius (86°F).

What are solids, liquids, and gases?

Envision It!

2.1.1 Observe, describe, and measure ways in which the properties of a sample of water (including volume) change or stay the same as it is heated and cooled and is transformed into different states. (Also 2.NS.2, 2.NS.3)

Circle three solids. **Draw** an ✗ on three liquids.

Inquiry Explore It!

How can water change?

☐ **1.** Put water in a cup. Ask your teacher to mark the water line.

☐ **2.** Put the cup in a freezer. Wait 1 day.

☐ **3.** Look at the line. Look at the top of the ice. **Record** your **observation.**

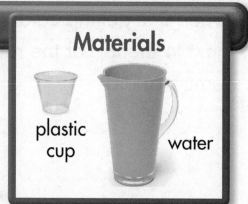

Materials

plastic cup

water

Explain Your Results

4. Predict What might happen if the ice melted?

2.NS.2 Conduct investigations that may happen over time as a class, in small groups, or independently.

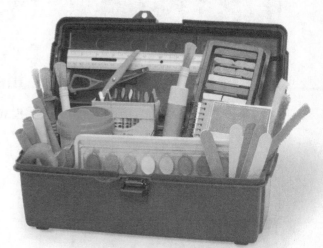

I will know that matter can be a solid, a liquid, or a gas.

Words to Know
....
solid
liquid
gas

Solids

Everything around you is made of matter. Three states of matter are solids, liquids, and gases.

A **solid** is matter that keeps its own size and shape. Solids take up space and have weight. Look at the picture. Each object in the box keeps its own size and shape.

Underline three states of matter.

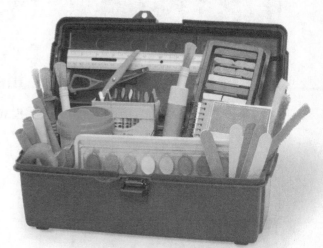

This art box and the objects in it are solids.

Draw one more solid that might go in the art box.

85

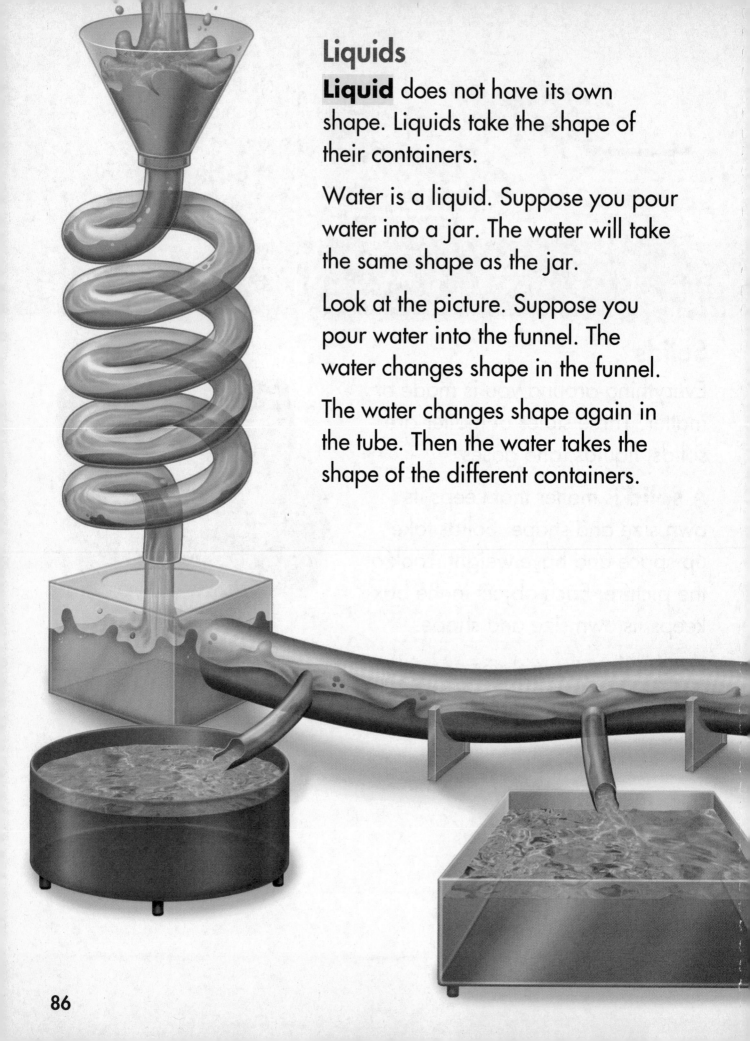

Liquids

Liquid does not have its own shape. Liquids take the shape of their containers.

Water is a liquid. Suppose you pour water into a jar. The water will take the same shape as the jar.

Look at the picture. Suppose you pour water into the funnel. The water changes shape in the funnel.

The water changes shape again in the tube. Then the water takes the shape of the different containers.

Write how solids and liquids are different.

_____
_____
_____
_____
_____

At-Home Lab

Water and Ice
Put some ice cubes in a bowl. Fill the bowl with water. Tell what happened to the solid. Tell what happened to the liquid.

Look at the picture. **Draw** two shapes the water takes.

Gases

Gas is matter. Gas does not have its own size or shape. Gas takes the size and shape of what it is in. Gas takes up all of the space inside its container. The bubbles in the picture are filled with gas.

You know that air is all around you. Air is made of gases that you cannot see.

How are liquids and gases alike?

_____

_____

_____

_____

_____

Where is the gas in this bouncer?

_____

_____

_____

Draw an arrow to the gas in a bubble.

Tell what shape the gas takes.

89

How can water change?

Envision It!

2.1.1 Observe, describe, and measure ways in which the properties of a sample of water (including volume) change or stay the same as it is heated and cooled and is transformed into different states. (Also 2.NS.2, 2.NS.3)

Tell how the ice is changing.

Inquiry **Explore It!**

How much water is in each cup?

Materials

crayon

3 plastic measuring cups (one with colored water)

☑ **1.** There is _____ mL in the first cup.

☑ **2.** Pour the liquid into another cup. **Measure. Record** your data.

How Much Water

— 250 mL — 200 mL — 150 mL — 100 mL — 50 mL	— 250 mL — 200 mL — 150 mL — 100 mL — 50 mL	— 250 mL — 200 mL — 150 mL — 100 mL — 50 mL
mL	mL	mL

Explain Your Results

3. Observe How did the volume and shape of the water change?

_____

_____

2.NS.2 Conduct investigations that may happen over time as a class, in small groups, or independently. **2.NS.6** Make and use simple equipment and tools to gather data and extend the senses.

Words to Know

volume

evaporate

Changing Shape

Matter can be changed. Water is matter. You can change the shape of water.

Suppose you pour a cup of water into a tall, thin container. The shape of the water will change. It looks like there is more liquid. However, the volume of the liquid is the same. **Volume** is the amount of space matter takes up. The volume of a liquid stays the same when it is poured into different kinds of containers.

Look at the pictures. **Tell** what shape the water takes.

The same amount of water was used to fill each of these containers.

91

Cooling Matter

Water can be a solid, a liquid, or a gas. Cooling can change the state of matter. Some properties of water change when it is cooled.

Water can change from a liquid to a solid. Suppose the air temperature is very cold. Rain will freeze and change to ice. Ice is a solid. The volume of ice is greater than the volume of liquid water.

Water can change from a gas to a liquid too. Have you ever had a cold drink on a hot day? Water vapor in the air touches the cold glass. The water vapor changes from a gas to a liquid. Tiny drops of water form on the glass.

Write how the properties of ice and liquid water are different.

Water on these leaves changed from a liquid to a solid. Water expands, or gets bigger, as it freezes.

Water vapor in the air changes into tiny drops of water on the glass.

Lightning Lab

Freeze Water
Put water in a clear plastic cup. Draw a line at the top of the water. Measure the mass. Freeze it. See if the volume or mass changed.

Heating Matter

Heating can change the state of matter. Some properties of water change when it is heated.

Ice and snow melt when the air warms. The volume of ice and snow gets smaller and smaller. Solid water becomes liquid water.

Puddles evaporate into the air. Water **evaporates** when it changes from a liquid to a gas. The liquid water in a puddle changes to water vapor. Water vapor is a gas. The volume of liquid water in the puddle gets smaller and smaller.

Suppose the temperature of water is very hot. Water boils and changes to water vapor. Water vapor is inside the bubbles of the boiling water.

○ **Draw Conclusions Look** at the pictures of the snowman. **Write** how the snow changed.

_____

_____

_____

_____

The water in the puddles will change into water vapor.

Draw an arrow to show where the water goes when it evaporates.

Label the water as a solid, a liquid, or a gas. **Tell** about the water in each picture.

_____

_____

_____

_____

_____

_____

95

What are mixtures?

2.1.2 Predict the result of combining solids and liquids in pairs. Mix, observe, gather, record and discuss evidence that the result may be a material with different properties than the original materials. **2.1.3** Predict and experiment with methods (e.g. sieving, evaporation) to separate solids and liquids based on their physical properties. (Also **2.NS.2 2.NS.3 2.NS.4**)

Circle the mixtures.

Inquiry Explore It!

How does a filter work?

☑ **1.** Put a filter on a cup. Use a rubber band.

☑ **2.** Put water in the other cup. Add 1 spoon of sand. Stir.

☑ **3.** Pour the mixture into the cup with the filter.

☑ **4. Observe** What happened?

Materials

sand   spoon

2 cups   water

coffee filter and rubber band

Explain Your Results

5. Infer How did the filter work?

2.NS.2 Conduct investigations that may happen over time as a class, in small groups, or independently. **2.NS.5** Discuss observations with peers and be able to support your conclusion with evidence.

UNLOCK THE BIG ?

I will know that properties of matter can change in a mixture. I will know that mixtures can be separated.

Words to Know

mixture
dissolve

Mixtures

You can stir matter together to make a mixture. A **mixture** is something made up of two or more kinds of matter. This fruit salad is a mixture of different kinds of fruit.

You can separate a mixture to see its parts. Suppose you separate the fruits in the salad. Each piece of fruit will stay the same.

Separate this mixture into its parts. **Draw** each part on its own plate.

97

Mix Solids and Liquids

Solids and liquids can be combined to make a mixture. Some materials change when they are mixed. Other materials stay the same.

Look at the picture of the ocean. The properties of sand and water stay the same when they are mixed.

Look at the picture of the lemonade. Lemonade can be made with lemons, sugar, and water. Sugar is a solid. It dissolves in water. **Dissolve** means to spread throughout a liquid. Sugar breaks up into tiny parts and becomes part of the liquid. The properties of sugar and water change when they are mixed.

Write solid or liquid to label the water, sugar, and lemonade. (Circle) the mixture.

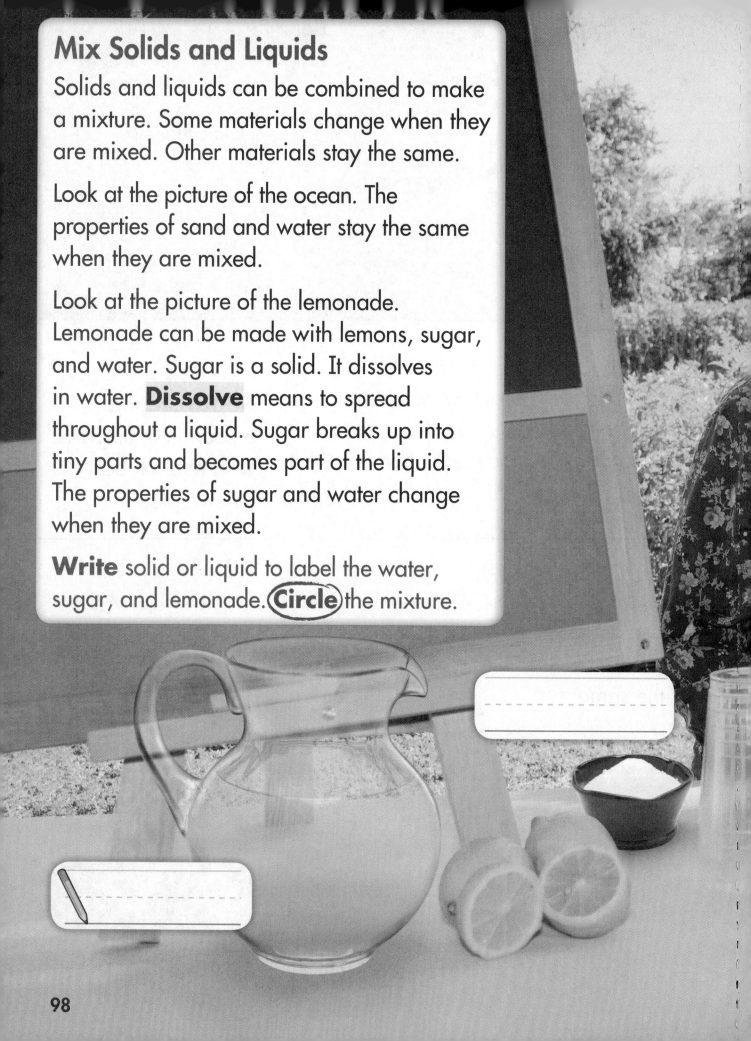

There is sand, salt, and water in the ocean. The salt is dissolved in the water. The sand sinks to the bottom of the ocean.

You cannot see the sugar in the lemonade. The sugar has changed.

Tell a property of sugar that changed.

Separate Mixtures

Mixtures can be separated in different ways. Think about a mixture of sand and water. The sand sinks to the bottom.

You can use a screen to separate a mixture of small rocks and water. A screen is a tool that can separate solids from liquids.

Suppose you mix sugar and water together. Then you let the water evaporate. Water evaporates when it changes from a liquid to a gas. You cannot separate a sugar-and-water mixture by letting sugar sink to the bottom of a container. You cannot use a screen to separate sugar and water either.

Look at the pictures.
Complete the sentences.

You can see the sugar after the water _____.

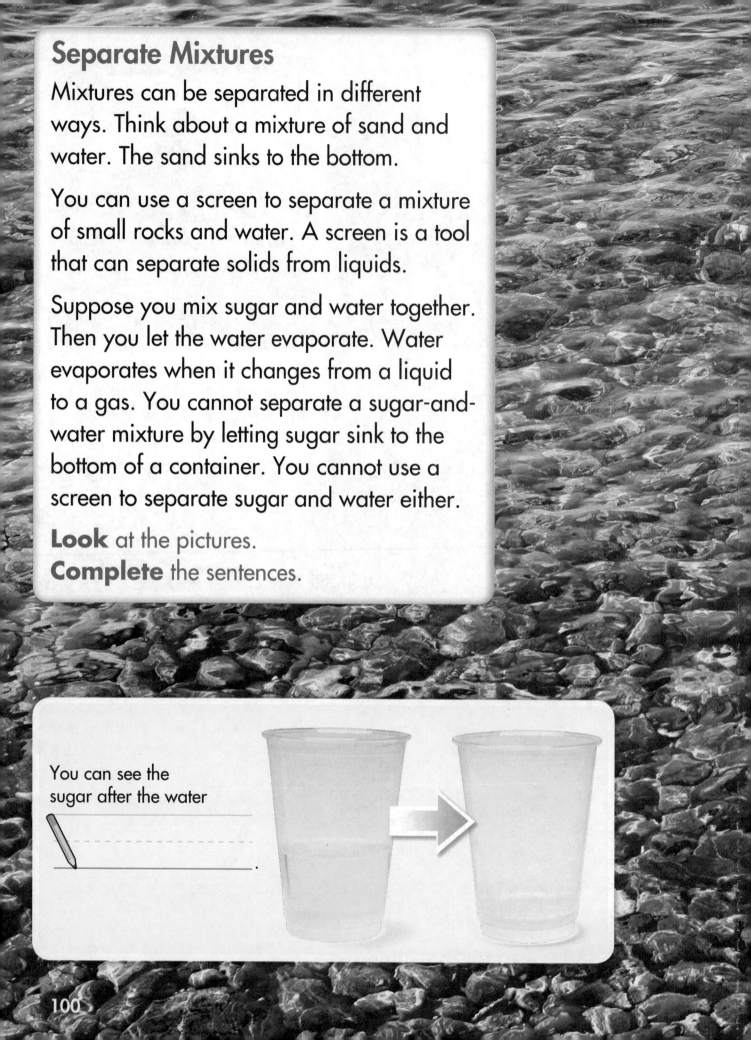

A screen can be used to
_____
_____
some solids from liquids.

water

sand

Draw the sand and water after they are mixed.

Draw the sand and water after they have separated.

How can properties change?

Follow a Procedure

☑ **1.** Put 30 mL of glue in a measuring cup. **Observe** the properties of the glue. **Record.**

Materials

measuring cup

safety goggles

spoon

water

borax solution

glue and food coloring

Substance Observations

Property	Glue	New Substance
Color		
Texture		
State of Matter (solid, liquid, gas)		

Inquiry Skill
After making an observation you can **record** your data in a chart.

☑ **2.** Add two drops of food coloring.

 Be careful! Wear safety goggles.

1 cc = 1 mL

🔵 **2.1.2** Predict the result of combining solids and liquids in pairs. Mix, observe, gather, record and discuss evidence that the result may be a material with different properties than the original materials. (Also **2.NS.1**)

☐ **3.** Add 15 mL of water to the cup.
Stir the mixture. Observe its properties.

☐ **4.** Add 15 mL of borax solution.
Stir. Observe what happens.

☐ **5.** Observe the new substance.
Investigate its properties.
Record your observations.

Be careful! Wash your hands when finished.

Analyze and Conclude

6. Compare the glue and the new substance.
How are the properties different?

_____

_____

_____

7. **UNLOCK THE BIG ?** **Infer** Would the new substance
be a good glue? Explain.

_____

_____

_____

Glassblower

Glass is a solid. Cool glass is hard. Heat makes glass hot and soft. Glass can be shaped to form different objects when it is soft. Glass becomes hard again when it cools.

Glassblowers use glass to make things like bowls and vases. Glassblowers put hot glass at one end of a long tube. They blow into the other end. Then they use tools to shape the glass.

You can see this colorful glass sculpture at the Children's Museum of Indianapolis. It was made by Dale Chihuly.

How does glass change when it is heated?

Vocabulary Smart Cards

matter
property
thermometer
solid
liquid
gas
volume
evaporate
mixture
dissolve

Play a Game!

Cut out the cards.

Work with a partner.

Cover up the words on each card.

Have your partner look at the picture and guess the word.

105

solid

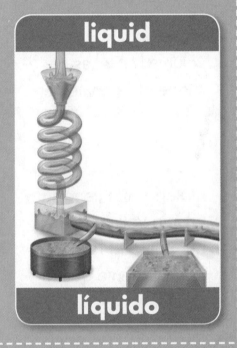

sólido

matter

materia

liquid

líquido

property

propiedad

gas

gas

thermometer

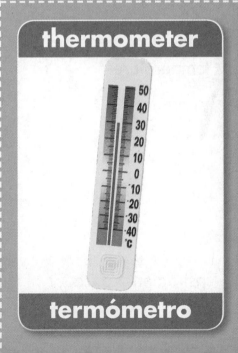

termómetro

anything that takes up space and has mass

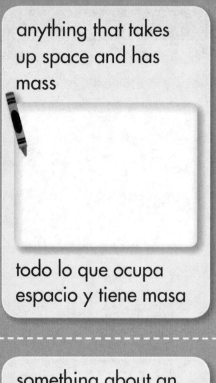

todo lo que ocupa espacio y tiene masa

matter that keeps its own size and shape

materia que mantiene tamaño y forma propios

something about an object that you can observe with your senses

algo en un objeto que puedes observar con tus sentidos

matter that has its own volume but takes the shape of its container

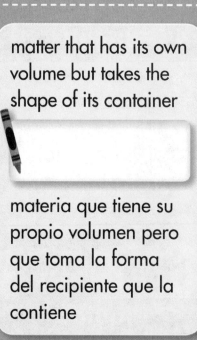

materia que tiene su propio volumen pero que toma la forma del recipiente que la contiene

a tool that measures temperature

instrumento para medir la temperatura

matter that does not have its own size or shape

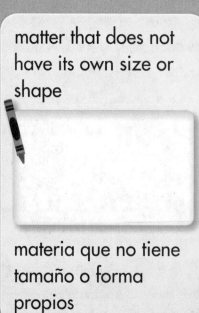

materia que no tiene tamaño o forma propios

 106

dissolve

disolver

volume

volumen

evaporate

evaporarse

mixture

mezcla

the amount of space
matter takes up

cantidad de espacio
que ocupa la materia

to spread throughout
a liquid

combinar una o más
sustancias en un
líquido

to change from a
liquid to a gas

cambiar de líquido a
gas

something made up
of two or more kinds
of matter

algo formado por
varios tipos de
materia

Lesson 1
What are some properties of matter?

- Temperature, weight, texture, and sinking or floating are properties of matter.

Lesson 2
What are solids, liquids, and gases?

- Solids keep their own shape. Liquids and gases take the shape of their containers.

Lesson 3
How can water change?

- Water can be a solid, a liquid, or a gas.
- Volume is the amount of space matter takes up.

Lesson 4
What are mixtures?

- Mixtures are made of different kinds of matter.
- Some materials change when they are mixed.

Lesson 1 2.1.1, 2.NS.3, 2.NS.4, 2.NS.5, 2.NS.6

1. Vocabulary Write two things you know about matter.

_____

_____

_____

2. Evaluate Circle two objects that have a property that is the same. **Tell** about your answer.

Lesson 2 2.1.1, 2.NS.2, 2.NS.3

3. Classify Circle the solids. **Draw** an ✕ on the liquid.

4. Vocabulary Which state of matter takes up all the space inside its container? **Circle** the letter.

A. solid   C. gas

B. liquid   D. property

Lesson 3
2.1.1, 2.NS.2, 2.NS.3

5. Describe How are water and water vapor different?

_____

_____

_____

6. Vocabulary Complete the sentence.

The _____ of water increases when it freezes.

Lesson 4
2.1.2, 2.1.3, 2.NS.2, 2.NS.3, 2.NS.4

◉ 7. Draw Conclusions You cannot see the sugar in the lemonade. **Write** what happened to the sugar.

_____

_____

Got it?

☐ Stop! I need help with _____

_____

▷ Go! Now I know _____

What makes roller coasters fun?

Force and Motion

 Try It! How much force does it take to move objects?

Lesson 1 What are motion and position?
2.1.4, 2.1.5

Lesson 2 What is force?
2.1.6, 2.NS.2, 2.NS.5

Lesson 3 What are magnets?
2.1.7, 2.NS.2, 2.NS.3, 2.NS.5

Lesson 4 What is gravity?
2.1.7, 2.NS.2, 2.NS.4

Investigate It! How high will a ball bounce?

Trace the path of the roller coaster with your finger. **Tell** how the roller coaster moves.

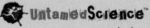 **How do forces make objects move?**

Go to www.myscienceonline.com and click on:

Untamed Science
Sing and dance to an Ecogeek music video!

Got it? 60-Second Video
Lesson reviewed in a minute!

I Will Know...
See what you've learned about science.

my pLaneT DiaRY
Connect to the world!

How much force does it take to move objects?

A force is a push or a pull. Force can be measured.

Be careful! Wear your safety goggles!

Materials

safety goggles

2 books

string

metric ruler

materials that stretch

☑ **1.** Pick a material. Find a way to **measure** how much force it takes to move a book. **Record.**

☑ **2.** Measure the force needed to move 2 books. Record.

Inquiry Skill
You **measure** when you compare the length of something to the ruler.

Explain Your Results

3. Explain how you **measured** force.

2.1.6 Observe, demonstrate, sketch, and compare how applied force (push or pull) changes the motion of objects. **2.NS.6** Make and use simple equipment and tools to gather data and extend the senses. (Also **2.1.4**, **2.NS.1**)

⊙ Cause and Effect

A **cause** is what makes something happen. An **effect** is what happens.

Practice It!

This boy is playing baseball. The boy swings the bat. The boy hits the ball. The ball goes far.
Write the effect of the boy hitting the ball.

Cause

The boy hits the ball.

Effect

115

What are motion and position?

2.1.4 Observe, sketch, demonstrate, and compare how objects can move in different ways (straight, zig-zag, back-and-forth, rolling, fast and slow). 2.1.5 Describe the position or motion of an object relative to a point of reference (background or another object).

Envision It!

Draw an arrow to show which way the rope is moving.

my planet Diary

Connections

Read Together

The ancient Egyptians built these pyramids a long time ago. The ancient Egyptians lived before trucks and cranes. It was hard to move the heavy stones they needed.

The ancient Egyptians were good problem solvers. They may have pushed the heavy stones up dirt ramps. They moved the stones all the way to the top of the pyramids!

How might the pyramids be built today?

UNLOCK
THE BIG
?
I will know that objects can move in different ways. I will know how to describe position.

Words to Know

motion

position

Motion

Motion is the act of moving. Objects can move in different ways. Objects can roll. They can move back and forth and fast and slow. Suppose you push a toy truck across the floor. The truck moves in a straight line.

You may move the truck in a zigzag motion. This means you push the truck one way and then another way.

Demonstrate how the merry-go-round moves.

Draw lines to show how the shoelaces were moved in a zigzag motion.

117

Lightning Lab

Position Words

Work in a group. Think of words that describe position. Write the words on cards. Put the cards in a pile. Pick one card. Use an object to demonstrate the word.

Position

You can use words to describe the position of an object. **Position** is where an object or person is. The words left and right describe position.

Look at the picture of the playground. You can use an object that does not move to tell position. The slide does not move. A boy is to the left of the slide.

Underline words that can help you describe position.

The bars are to the right of the slide.

Describe Position

You can use words like in front of, next to, and behind to help you describe position too.

Look at the picture of the people gardening. You can see that the girl is behind the flowers.

You can use things in the background to help you describe position. The tree is in the background. The girl is in front of the tree.

(Circle) something that is behind the woman.

Describe the position of the green watering can.

The girl and the woman are next to each other.

Draw two objects. **Describe** their positions.

What is force?

Envision It!

2.1.6 Observe, demonstrate, sketch, and compare how applied force (push or pull) changes the motion of objects. (Also 2.NS.2, 2.NS.5)

Circle the ball you need to hit with greater force to get it in the hole.

Inquiry **Explore It!**

What can you do to move objects?

□ **1.** Use a straw to blow once on each ball.

Blow the same way both times.

Materials

straw

table tennis ball

rubber ball

meterstick

□ **2. Measure** how far the balls move.

rubber ball _____

table tennis ball _____

Explain Your Results

Be careful! Do not share straws.

3. Communicate How can you make a ball move?

_____

_____

4. Interpret Data Which ball is harder to move? Why?

_____

_____

_____

2.1.4 Observe, sketch, demonstrate, and compare how objects can move in different ways (straight, zig-zag, back-and-forth, rolling, fast and slow). (Also **2.1.5, 2.NS.1**)

UNLOCK THE BIG ?

I will know that the way an object moves depends on the amount and direction of force that is used.

Word to Know

force

Force

You can move things in different ways. A push or a pull that makes something move is called a **force.** A force changes the way an object moves.

An object will change its motion in the direction it is pushed or pulled. Suppose you change the direction of the force. The object will move in a different direction.

Someone kicks a ball to you. The ball changes direction when you kick it back.

◎ **Cause and Effect** The man throws the ball. The boy throws it back. **Draw** an arrow to show the new direction.

121

Fast and Slow

The speed of an object depends on the amount of force used. Speed is how fast or slow an object moves.

Suppose an object is not moving. A force will make the object start to move. The object will move faster if you apply more force. You apply more force when you push or pull harder. The object will move slower if you apply less force.

A bicycle will move slower if you apply less force on the pedals.

Lightning Lab

Flight Path
Make a paper airplane. Throw it softly. Watch it fly. Tell how far it flew. Throw the paper airplane hard. Tell how far it flew. Compare how the amount of force changed the distance your plane flew.

You pull a wagon. **Write** how you can make the wagon go faster.

Far and Near

How far an object moves depends on how much force is used. It takes more force to move objects farther.

Suppose you wanted to make a soccer ball go far. Kick it hard. You have used more force. Watch how far it goes!

Suppose you wanted to make a soccer ball roll a little bit. Tap it! You have used less force. It will not move far.

Cause and Effect You push a block across the floor. **Write** how the amount of force can change how far the block moves.

Lesson 3

What are magnets?

2.1.7 Investigate the motion of objects when they are acted upon by forces at a distance such as gravity and magnetism. (Also 2.NS.2, 2.NS.3, 2.NS.5)

Envision It!

Why do the letters stay on the refrigerator?

Inquiry Explore It!

What can a magnet pull through?

☐ **1.** Put a paper clip in a cup. Hold the magnet as shown.

☐ **2.** **Record** what you **observe.**

Materials

magnet

paper square

paper clip

plastic cup

plastic cup with water

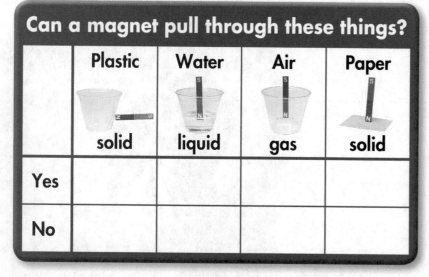

Can a magnet pull through these things?

	Plastic solid	Water liquid	Air gas	Paper solid
Yes				
No				

Explain Your Results

3. Interpret Data What can the magnet pull through?

_____

_____

2.NS.2 Conduct investigations that may happen over time as a class, in small groups, or independently. (Also **2.1.6, 2.NS.1**)

They are ___ ___ ___ ___ ___ ___ ___.

UNLOCK THE BIG ?

I will know that magnets can push or pull some metal objects.

Words to Know

attract

repel

Magnets

Magnets can push or pull some metal objects.

Magnets attract some metal objects. **Attract** means to pull toward.

Magnets can repel other magnets. **Repel** means to push away.

The ability to attract and repel objects is a property of matter.

◉ **Cause and Effect** (Circle) the objects that are attracted to the magnet. **Draw** an X on the objects that are not attracted.

Tell why some of the objects were not attracted to the magnet.

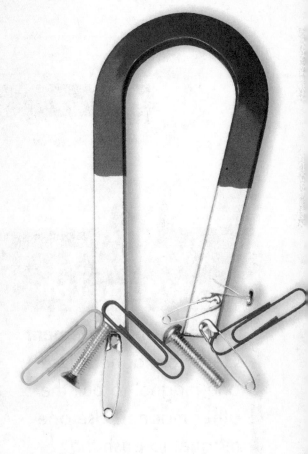

125

Magnet Poles

Magnets have poles. A pole is the place on a magnet that has the strongest push or pull. Look at the poles of the magnets. The N stands for north pole. The S stands for south pole.

Put like poles together.
They repel each other.

Put opposite poles together.
They attract each other.

At-Home Lab

Magnets and Movement
Get two magnets. Use one magnet to pull the other magnet. Use one magnet to push the other magnet. Tell what happens when you try to put the two magnets together.

Write why the north and south poles are attracted to each other.

How Magnets Move Objects

A magnet can move some things without touching them. Look at the picture below. The spoon is moving toward the magnet. The magnet is not touching the spoon. The force of the magnet pulls the spoon.

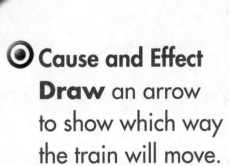

⊙ **Cause and Effect**
Draw an arrow to show which way the train will move.

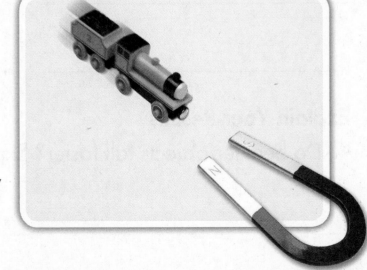

What is gravity?

2.1.7 Investigate the motion of objects when they are acted upon by forces at a distance such as gravity and magnetism. (Also **2.NS.2**, **2.NS.4**)

Draw a line to show how the basketball will move.

Inquiry **Explore It!**

How do heavier objects fall?

☑ **1.** Put 5 marbles in one bag.
Put 10 in another. Seal the bags.

☑ **2.** Hold both bags at the same height.
Drop them at the same time.
Repeat 3 times.

☑ **3.** **Record** your **observations.**

Materials

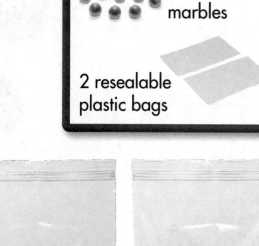

15 metal marbles

2 resealable plastic bags

Explain Your Results

4. Do heavier objects fall faster? Explain using your **observations.**

2.1.6 Observe, demonstrate, sketch, and compare how applied force (push or pull) changes the motion of objects. (Also **2.NS.3**)

UNLOCK
THE BIG
?

I will know that gravity pulls things toward the center of Earth.

Word to Know

gravity

Gravity

Gravity is a pulling force. Gravity pulls things toward the center of Earth. Look at the girl jumping in the air. She will not float up. Gravity will pull her down.

Think about when it rains. Gravity is the force that pulls the rain down to the ground.

◎ **Cause and Effect Write** what would happen if gravity did not pull on the leaves in the picture.

_____

_____

_____

_____

Gravity and Weight

Look at the girl playing with the toy. Gravity is pulling the toy down. Gravity pulls things toward the ground unless something holds them up.

How much something weighs tells how strong the pull of gravity is on it. The table weighs more than the toy drum. The pull of gravity is stronger on the table than on the toy drum.

Draw an arrow to show how the toy moves because of gravity.

130

Write why the toy bear does not fall to the ground.

Write whether the pull of gravity is stronger on the girl or on the balls. **Tell** how you know.

![Lightning Lab icon]

Lightning Lab

Sink or Float
Make a boat using foil. Put the boat in a bowl of water. Add pennies one at a time. Tell how many pennies you added before the boat sank.

131

How high will a ball bounce?

Follow a Procedure

☑ **1.** Tape a meterstick to a wall.

Drop the ball from 50 cm.

Measure how high it bounces.

Record.

_____ cm

☑ **2.** Repeat, but drop
from 100 cm.

_____ cm

Materials
meterstick

tape   rubber ball

safety goggles

Inquiry Skill
Constructing a bar graph
can help you collect,
record, and **interpret data.**

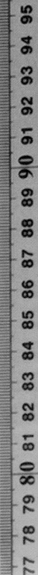

⬤ 2.1.4 Observe, sketch, demonstrate, and compare how objects can move in different ways (straight, zig-zag, back-and-forth, rolling, fast and slow).
2.1.5 Describe the position or motion of an object relative to a point of reference (background or another object). (Also **2.1.6, 2.1.7, 2.NS.3**)

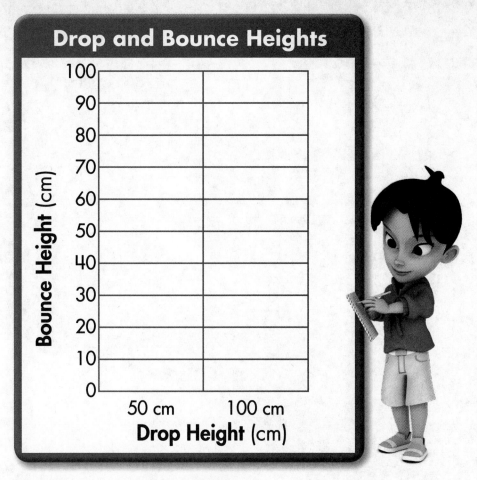

Drop and Bounce Heights

Bounce Height (cm)

100
90
80
70
60
50
40
30
20
10
0

50 cm   100 cm

Drop Height (cm)

Analyze and Conclude

3. Interpret Data When did the ball bounce higher?

_____

_____

4. Infer What force pulled the ball to the ground?

_____

_____

5. **UNLOCK THE BIG ?** How did the height you dropped the ball from affect how high the ball bounced?

_____

_____

_____

_____

Bike Riding

Riding a bike is a lot of fun. Riding a bike helps Earth too! Riding a bike does not cause air pollution.

You can ride bikes with your family at the Harmonie Hundred in New Harmony, Indiana. Many people enjoy this tour, which includes a short ride through Harmonie State Park.

Riders use force to make their bikes move. Riders use a lot of force to ride fast.

Write how riders use force to make their bikes move fast.

134

Vocabulary Smart Cards

- motion
- position
- force
- attract
- repel
- gravity

Play a Game!

Cut out the cards.

Work with a partner.

Pick a card.

Say clues about the word.

Have your partner guess the word.

attract

atraer

motion

movimiento

repel

repeler

position

posición

gravity

gravedad

force

fuerza

the act of moving

el acto de moverse

to pull toward

jalar hacia sí

where an object is

donde está un objeto

to push away

apartar algo
empujándolo

a push or pull that
makes something
move

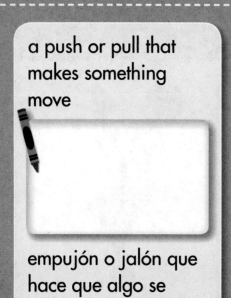

empujón o jalón que
hace que algo se
mueva

a force that pulls
things toward the
center of Earth

fuerza que jala los
objetos hacia el
centro de la Tierra

Chapter 4
Study Guide REVIEW THE BIG  How do forces make objects move?

Indiana

Lesson 1

What are motion and position?

- Motion is the act of moving.
- Position is where an object is.

Lesson 2

What is force?

- Force is a push or pull that makes objects move.
- Objects will move farther if more force is used.

Lesson 3

What are magnets?

- Magnets attract some objects and repel other objects.

Lesson 4

What is gravity?

- Gravity is a force that pulls objects toward the ground unless something holds them up.

Lesson 1 2.1.4, 2.1.5

1. Apply Draw lines to show two ways the car can move.

2. Describe Write about your position in the room. Use the words right, left, in front of, or behind.

Lesson 2 2.1.6, 2.NS.2, 2.NS.5

3. Vocabulary What is a push or a pull that makes something move? **Circle** the letter.

A. speed

C. position

B. force

D. repel

⊙ **4. Cause and Effect** **Circle** the kick that will make the ball go farther.

Lesson 3 ⏱ 2.1.7, 2.NS.2, 2.NS.3, 2.NS.5

5. Infer (Circle) the objects the magnet attracts.

6. Vocabulary Write the words attract and repel to complete the sentences.

Like poles _____ each other.

Opposite poles _____ each other.

Lesson 4 ⏱ 2.1.7, 2.NS.2, 2.NS.4

7. Infer Write why the girl does not fall to the ground.

_____

_____

_____

_____

Got it?

⏹ **Stop!** I need help with _____

_____

▶ **Go!** Now I know _____

How does a seesaw work?

Materials

toy car

eraser

pennies

ruler with plastic cups (prepared by teacher)

Ask a question.

How can a smaller person lift a bigger person on a seesaw? Use a ruler to find out.

Make a prediction.

1. If you move one cup closer to the middle of a ruler, will you need more or fewer pennies to lift the other cup?

(a) more pennies

(b) fewer pennies

Plan a fair test.

Use two cups that are the same size.

Inquiry Skill

You plan an **experiment** when you design a way to answer a scientific question.

Design your test.

☑ **2.** Make a seesaw model. Draw it in the chart.

☑ **3.** List your steps.

2.1.6 Observe, demonstrate, sketch, and compare how applied force (push or pull) changes the motion of objects. **2.NS.4** Make predictions based on observations. **2.NS.7** Recognize a fair test. (Also **2.DP.5, 2.DP.6, 2.DP.8**)

Do your test.

☑ **4.** Follow your steps.

Collect and record data.

☑ **5.** Fill in the chart.

Tell your conclusion.

6. When did you use fewer pennies?

_____

_____

7. Communicate   How can a smaller person
lift a bigger person on a seesaw?

_____

_____

_____

_____

Solids	Liquids	Gases

Make a Chart

- Make a chart with three columns.

- Label the columns Solids, Liquids, and Gases.

- Write words or draw pictures in the columns to show solids, liquids, and gases.

2.1.1

Write a Fable

- A fable is a story that is made up to teach a lesson.

- Write a fable that teaches a lesson about why everything that goes up must come down.

2.1.7

Changing Speed

- Find toy cars with wheels of different sizes.

- Find out how different sizes of wheels affect how fast toy cars can go.

2.1.6, 2.NS.2, 2.NS.7

Using Scientific Methods

1. Ask a question.

2. Make a hypothesis.

3. Plan a fair test.

4. Do your test.

5. Collect and record data.

6. Tell your conclusion.

Earth Science

Chapter 5
Earth and Sky

 How does weather change over time?

When can you see a rainbow?

Earth and Sky

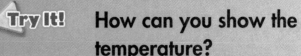

Try It! How can you show the temperature?

Investigate It! What is your weather like?

Tell what the weather is like when you can see a rainbow.

How does weather change over time?

Go to www.myscienceonline.com and click on:

UntamedScience™
Watch the Ecogeeks in this wild video.

Got it? **60-Second Video**
Watch and learn.

Envision It!
Interact with science to find out what you know.

Vocabulary Smart Cards
Mix and match vocabulary practice!

Materials

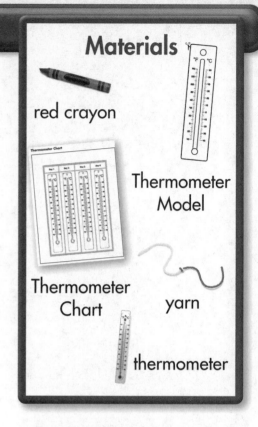

red crayon

Thermometer Model

Thermometer Chart

yarn

thermometer

How can you show the temperature?

☑ **1.** Use the Thermometer Model. Put each end of your yarn through the holes in front of your model.

☑ **2.** Your teacher will tell you the temperature. Move the yarn up or down to show the temperature.

☑ **3.** Use a real thermometer. **Measure** the temperature outside. **Record** on the Thermometer Chart.

☑ **4.** Repeat for 3 more days.

Inquiry Skill You can use a thermometer to **measure** temperature.

Explain Your Results

5. Tell about the changes in temperature you **measured.**

_____

_____

_____

_____

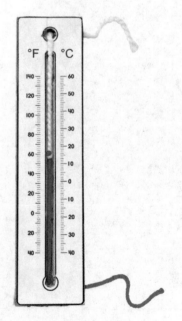

2.2.1 Construct and use tools to observe and measure weather phenomena such as precipitation, changes in temperature, wind speed and direction.
2.2.3 Chart or graph weather observations such as cloud cover, cloud type, and type of precipitation on a daily basis over a period of weeks.

Compare and Contrast

Compare means to tell how things are alike. **Contrast** means to tell how things are different.

Spring and Winter

Spring can be warm. Spring can be windy. Spring is sometimes very rainy. Winter can be cold. Winter can be windy. Winter can be snowy too.

Practice It!

Compare and **contrast** spring and winter.

Compare	Contrast

What is weather?

2.2.1 Construct and use tools to observe and measure weather phenomena such as precipitation, changes in temperature, wind speed and direction. **2.2.2** Experience and describe wind (moving air) as motion of the air that surrounds us and takes up space. (Also **2.NS.1**, **2.NS.6**)

Envision It!

Tell what the weather is like in the picture.

Inquiry **Explore It!**

Which way does the wind blow?

☑ **1.** Label the plate **N, E, S,** and **W.** Add clay.

☑ **2.** Tape the tissue to the straw. Put the straw in the clay.

☑ **3.** **Observe** outside. What direction is the wind coming from?

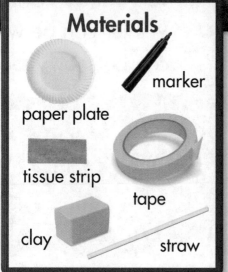

Materials

marker

paper plate

tissue strip

tape

clay

straw

_____

Explain Your Results

4. Compare with others. **Observe** again if different. Write.

_____

_____

_____

_____

2.NS.3 Generate questions and make observations about natural processes. **2.NS.6** Make and use simple equipment and tools to gather data and extend the senses. (Also **2.NS.5**)

UNLOCK THE BIG ? I will know how to measure different kinds of weather.

Word to Know

wind

Weather

Weather is what the air outside is like. Air is all around you. Air takes up space. Sometimes you can feel air moving. Moving air is called **wind.**

Scientists observe and measure weather to warn people about storms. An anemometer is a tool that measures the speed of wind. This tool helps scientists know when winds are dangerous.

Watch the tree branches. If the tree branches are moving, the wind is blowing.

◉ **Compare and Contrast Write** how the weather in the picture and the weather outside are alike and different.

Compare	Contrast

Tools for Measuring Weather

Tools help scientists study weather. Scientists use tools to measure temperature, wind, and rainfall.

A wind vane shows the direction of the wind. The wind vane points to where the wind is coming from.

A rain gauge measures how much rain has fallen. Raindrops fall into the gauge. Numbers tell the amount of rain in inches and centimeters.

A thermometer measures temperature. This thermometer shows the temperature in degrees Celsius and Fahrenheit.

Picture Clues What temperature is shown on the thermometer?

Predict Weather

Scientists gather weather information over many years. They learn what the weather of a place might be like at different times. They use this information to predict weather.

The graph shows rainfall for Indianapolis, Indiana. It tells how much rain fell in July over three years.

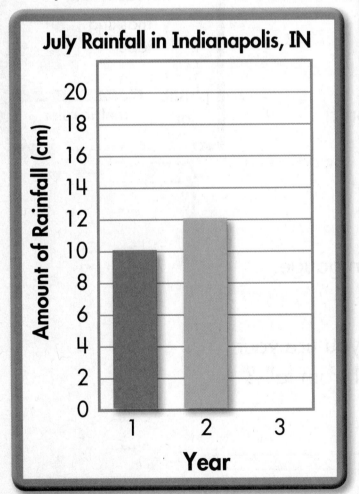

July Rainfall in Indianapolis, IN

At-Home Lab

Chart the Weather

Look at the weather report in the newspaper every day for a week. Record the temperature and wind speed. Put a thermometer outside. Check it every day at the same time for a week. Compare the temperature information from both sources.

Draw a bar on the graph to show that it rained 10 centimeters in Year 3.

Tell which year had the most rainfall. How much rain fell?

151

Lesson 2

How does weather change?

2.2.4 Ask questions about charted observations and graphed data. Identify the patterns and cycles of weather day-to-day as well as seasonal time scales in terms of temperature and rainfall/snowfall amounts. (Also 2.NS.4)

Envision It!

spring   summer

Color the trees to show what they look like in each season.

Inquiry Explore It!

How much rain falls?

Make a rain gauge.

Materials

masking tape

plastic jar   metric ruler

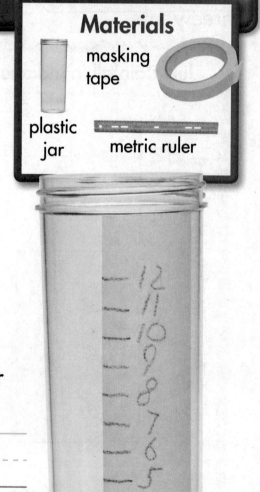

☑ 1. Make 12 lines 1 cm apart on a piece of tape.

☑ 2. Number the lines.

☑ 3. Fasten the tape to the jar.

☑ 4. Make a plan to use your rain gauge.

Explain Your Results

5. **Communicate** How could you use your rain gauge to find how much rain falls?

_____

_____

_____

_____

2.2.1 Construct and use tools to observe and measure weather phenomena such as precipitation, changes in temperature, wind speed and direction.
2.NS.6 Make and use simple equipment and tools to gather data and extend the senses.

fall   winter

Words to Know

pattern
precipitation

Weather Patterns

Weather follows a pattern. A **pattern** is the way something repeats itself.

Weather follows patterns from day to day. In many places, the temperature is cool in the morning. It is warmer in the afternoon. Often the temperature gets cool again at night.

Weather in many places changes with the seasons. The seasons are spring, summer, fall, and winter. The seasons repeat every year too.

Look at the picture.
Describe what you think the weather will be like tomorrow.
Tell how you know.

153

Spring and Summer

Some spring days are cool. Some are warm. Spring days can be rainy. Rain is a kind of precipitation. **Precipitation** is the water that falls to Earth. Buds and leaves begin to grow on plants during spring. Birds and other animals have babies.

Summer comes after spring. Some summer days are hot. The nights are often warm. Trees and other plants have lots of green leaves. Flowers bloom, and many fruits and vegetables grow.

⊙ **Compare and Contrast Write** how temperature and precipitation in spring and summer are different where you live.

spring

summer

fall

winter

Fall and Winter

Fall comes after summer. Some fall days are warm. Some are cool. Many plants stop growing. Leaves change color and drop from some trees. Many animals store food for the coming winter.

Winter comes after fall. Winter in some places can be very cold and snowy. Water in ponds and lakes may freeze. Many trees have no leaves at all. Some animals hibernate, or sleep, all winter long.

⊚ **Compare and Contrast** **Tell** how fall and winter are different.

Lightning Lab

Changing Seasons
Make a chart. Name a season. Write three words that tell about the weather of your season. Tell what the weather is like before the season. Tell what the weather is like after the season.

What are clouds?

Envision It!

2.2.3 Chart or graph weather observations such as cloud cover, cloud type, and type of precipitation on a daily basis over a period of weeks. (Also 2.NS.1, 2.NS.4)

Describe these clouds.

my planet diary Did You Know?

Read Together

Rain and melted snow flow into lakes and other bodies of water. We get drinking water from some of these places. Did you know that we also get drinking water from under the ground?

Water from rain and snow soaks into the ground. It fills up spaces between rocks. This is called groundwater. People get this water out of the ground. Then it is purified, or made very clean. If you get water to drink from a faucet, you may drink groundwater!

What happens to water that soaks into the ground? **Underline** the sentence that tells you.

Clouds

Close your eyes and picture a cloud. What does it look like? Different kinds of clouds bring different kinds of weather. Some clouds are white and fluffy. These clouds are signs of fair weather. Other clouds are thick and dark. These clouds are signs of rain or snow.

Look at the picture of the clouds. **Predict** the weather. **Explain** your answer.

How Clouds Form

The sun heats the water from oceans, rivers, lakes, and ponds. Then the water evaporates. The water that evaporates changes to water vapor. **Water vapor** is a form of water in the air. You cannot see water vapor.

Water vapor moves high into the sky. The water vapor gets colder as it moves higher and higher. Very cold water vapor changes into tiny drops of water or ice. These drops make many different kinds of clouds. Big drops of water or ice can get too heavy to stay in the clouds. They fall from the clouds as rain.

Draw an X on clouds you might see on a rainy day.

(Circle) clouds you might see when the weather is fair.

cumulonimbus clouds

▲ These clouds are tall and dense. Heavy rain often comes from these kinds of clouds.

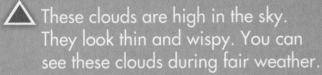
cirrus clouds

 These clouds are high in the sky. They look thin and wispy. You can see these clouds during fair weather.

At-Home Lab

A Week of Clouds
Make a chart. Look at clouds at the same time each day. How much of the sky is full of clouds? Record the cloud type.

These clouds are at all different heights in the sky. They look puffy. You can see these clouds in fair weather too. ▷

cumulus clouds

These clouds are low in the sky. They look flat and gray. You can see these clouds on cloudy days.
▽

stratus clouds

Write about the clouds today.

159

How can you stay safe in severe weather?

2.2.6 Learn about, report on, and practice severe weather safety procedures.

Tell what you think you should do if you see lightning.

Inquiry Explore It!

What do tornadoes look like?

☑ **1. Make a Model**   Put the tops of the bottles together. Seal with duct tape.

duct tape →

☑ **2.** Flip the bottles. The water is now on top.

☑ **3.** Swirl. **Observe** the top bottle.

Materials

empty plastic bottle

plastic bottle with water

duct tape

Explain Your Results

4. How is your model like a tornado? How is it different?

_____

_____

_____

_____

_____

2.NS.2 Conduct investigations that may happen over time as a class, in small groups, or independently. 2.NS.3 Generate questions and make observations about natural processes.

Words to Know

severe weather

Thunderstorms

A thunderstorm is one kind of severe weather. **Severe weather** is dangerous weather. A thunderstorm is heavy rain with thunder and lightning. Sometimes thunderstorms have hail and strong winds too.

Underline two details about thunderstorms.

Hail is pieces of ice that fall from clouds.

Thunderstorm Safety

- Find shelter in a sturdy building.
- Keep away from windows, water, and trees.
- Keep away from metal objects.
- Keep away from things that use electricity.

161

Tornadoes

Tornadoes can happen during thunderstorms. A tornado is a small but very strong wind that comes down from thunderstorm clouds.

Tornadoes form very quickly. It is hard to predict when tornadoes will happen. A tornado can destroy things in its path.

Write why it is important to be ready for severe weather.

_____

_____

_____

Tornado Safety

- Go to the basement or an inside room.

- Crouch under the stairs or near an inner wall.

- Stay away from windows.

- Cover your head.

Draw an X on the place where the tornado in this picture came down from.

At-Home Lab

Safe Places
Work with an adult. Identify one kind of severe weather. Make a plan to stay safe. Tell where safe places are. Tell what things you will need.

Hurricanes

A hurricane is a large storm that starts over warm ocean water. A hurricane has heavy rains. The rains can cause floods. A hurricane has very strong winds. The winds can knock down trees and buildings.

⊙ **Compare and Contrast Write** how tornadoes and hurricanes are alike and different.

_____

Hurricane Safety

- Move away from the ocean.

- Bring loose objects inside.

- Stay inside and away from windows.

- Store extra food and water in your home.

Draw an arrow to show which way the wind is blowing.

165

What does the sun do?

 2.2.5 Ask questions and design class investigations on the effect of the sun heating the surface of the earth. 2.2.7 Investigate how the sun appears to move through the sky during the day by observing and drawing the length and direction of shadows. (Also 2.NS.5 2.NS.6 2.NS.7)

Draw yourself at the beach.

Inquiry **Explore It!**

What can the sun's energy do?

☑ **1.** Tilt a solar collector toward the sun.

☑ **2.** Place a lump of clay near the bowl. Put a crayon into the clay.

☑ **3.** **Observe** both crayons after 10 minutes. Describe both crayons.

Materials

clay

solar collector with crayon

timer or stopwatch

unwrapped crayon

book

Explain Your Results

4. Infer   Explain your **observation.**

2.NS.2 Conduct investigations that may happen over time as a class, in small groups, or independently.

Tell why the sand gets so hot.

UNLOCK THE BIG ?

I will know that the sun warms the water, land, and air. I will know how shadows change during the day.

Word to Know

shadow

Light and Heat

The sun is important to all living things on Earth. Earth gets light from the sun. Light is one kind of energy. Light energy causes heat. Light energy from the sun warms the land, air, and water on Earth.

People and animals use sunlight to see in the daytime. Earth would stay dark without the sun.

Think about the air temperature during the summer and winter. What is one reason the air temperature might be different?

Energy from the sun warms the land, water, and air.

167

Sun in the Sky

The sun seems to move across the sky during the day. The sun looks low in the sky in the morning at sunrise. The sun is high in the sky at noon. It looks low in the sky again in the evening at sunset.

Label each picture. Write sunrise, noon, or sunset.

The sun does not really move across the sky. Earth moves. Each day, Earth spins around once. As Earth spins, the sun seems to be moving.

You may not see the sun on a cloudy day. The sun is behind the clouds. The sun always shines, even when you cannot see it.

Lightning Lab

Light and Heat
Fill two cups with soil. Place one in the sunlight. Place one in the shade. Wait 30 minutes. Measure the temperature of the soil in each cup. How are the temperatures different? Tell what caused the change.

Light and Shadows

You can see your shadow when your body blocks the sunlight. A **shadow** is the shape that is made when an object blocks the light. Shadows change during the day.

Shadows look long in early morning. Shadows look short by the middle of the day. Shadows look long again in the evening.

Suppose you are standing outside on a sunny day. The sun is high in the sky. **Draw** yourself and your shadow.

Shadows are long in the morning. They get shorter until noon.

Shadows are shortest at noon. Then they get longer until sunset.

Shadows are long again in the evening.

spring

fall

Season to Season

Shadows change from season to season. Every day during winter and spring, the path of the sun across the sky gets higher. Every day during summer and fall, the path of the sun across the sky gets lower.

Shadows are longer in fall and winter. Shadows are shorter in spring and summer.

Would your shadow be longer in fall or spring? **Write** how you know.

171

Lesson 6

How does the moon change?

2.2.8 Investigate how the moon appears to move through the sky during the day by observing and drawing its location at different times.
2.2.9 Investigate how the shape of the moon changes from day to day in a repeating cycle that lasts about a month. (Also 2.NS.1)

The moon is round. **Tell** why you think the moon looks like this.

Inquiry Explore It!

How does the shape of the moon appear to change?

☑ **1.** Use the Moon Calendar Sheet.

☑ **2. Observe** the moon every night.

☑ **3. Record data** by drawing pictures on the calendar.

Materials

Moon Calendar Sheet

markers

Explain Your Results

4. Communicate Describe how the moon changed.

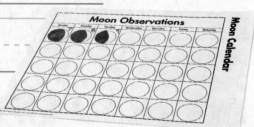

2.NS.1 Use a scientific notebook to record predictions, questions and observations about data with pictures, numbers or in words. **2.NS.2** Conduct investigations that may happen over time as a class, in small groups, or independently.

Words to Know

reflect
crater
phase

Moon

Think of the sky at night. The moon looks like the biggest and brightest object in the night sky. The moon does not make its own light. It reflects light from the sun. **Reflect** means to bounce off.

The moon is round like Earth. The moon is much smaller than Earth. The moon is made of rock. It has mountains and deep craters. A **crater** is a hole in the ground shaped like a bowl.

Draw an X on a crater.
Describe the moon.

A crater forms when a large rock from space hits the moon.

Moon at Night

The moon moves in a path around Earth. It takes about four weeks for the moon to go once around Earth. The moon seems to change shape as it moves.

Sometimes the moon looks round. This is called a full moon. Sometimes you see smaller parts of the moon. Sometimes you cannot see the moon at all.

Sometimes you can see the moon during the day. However, it is harder to notice when the sun is out.

Look at the pictures of the moon. **Draw** an X on the full moon.

Phases of the Moon

Why does the shape of the moon seem to change? Remember that the moon reflects light from the sun. You only see the part of the moon that has light shining on it. The shape of the lighted part of the moon is called a **phase.**

Write why the moon seems to change shape.

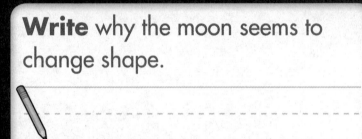

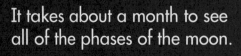

It takes about a month to see all of the phases of the moon.

Moon in the Sky

Earth spins around once every day. Because
Earth spins, the moon seems to move across
the sky. The moon seems to move across the
sky in the same direction as the sun.

Underline why you can see
the moon move across the sky.

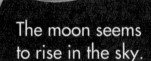

The moon seems
to rise in the sky.

Position of the Moon

Look at the moon at the same time every
night. You can see the position of the moon
in the sky change. This happens because
the moon moves around Earth.

The moon seems to rise and set later and
later every day. After four weeks, you
can see the moon at the same time and
place again.

Tell why the position of the moon in the
sky changes from night to night.

What is your weather like?

Follow a Procedure

☑ **1.** Put the weather tools outside.

☑ **2.** Check the tools at the same time each day for 5 days.

☑ **3. Measure** and **record** your data.

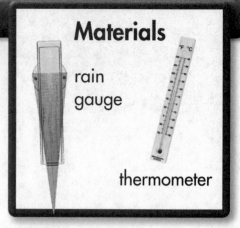

Materials

rain gauge

thermometer

Inquiry Skill
Data you collect can be **recorded** in a chart.

2.2.1 Construct and use tools to observe and measure weather phenomena such as precipitation, changes in temperature, wind speed and direction.
2.2.3 Chart or graph weather observations such as cloud cover, cloud type, and type of precipitation on a daily basis over a period of weeks.
(Also 2.2.4, 2.NS.6)

Rain and Temperature Observations

Day of the Week	Rain (cm)	Temperature (°C)
Monday		
Tuesday		
Wednesday		
Thursday		
Friday		

Analyze and Conclude

4. **UNLOCK THE BIG ?** **Classify** the days as rainy or not rainy.

Rainy _____

_____

Not Rainy _____

5. Tell about the temperature over the 5 days.

_____

_____

6. Tell how the weather changed over the 5 days.

_____

_____

Indiana State Climate Office

Scientists learn about Indiana's weather at the Indiana State Climate Office at Purdue University in West Lafayette. They learn how hot or cold it is. They learn how much rain falls. Scientists keep track of the weather patterns in Indiana.

Keep a record of the weather for three days. **Measure** the temperature at the same time each day. **Write** if it is sunny, rainy, or windy. **Find** a pattern.

Big World

	What is the temperature?	Is it sunny, rainy, or windy?
Day 1		
Day 2		
Day 3		

My World

Tell what you think the weather will be on Day 4.

Vocabulary Smart Cards

wind

pattern

precipitation

water vapor

severe
 weather

shadow

reflect

crater

phase

Play a Game!

Cut out the cards.

Work with a partner.

Cover up the words on each card.

Have your partner look at the picture and guess the word.

181

water vapor

vapor de agua

wind

viento

severe weather

tiempo severo

pattern

patrón

shadow

sombra

precipitation

precipitación

moving air

aire que se mueve

a form of water in the air

una forma del agua en el aire

the way something repeats itself

la manera en que algo se repite

dangerous weather

tiempo peligroso

the water that falls to Earth

el agua que cae a la Tierra

the shape that is made when an object blocks the light

forma que se ve cuando un objeto bloquea la luz

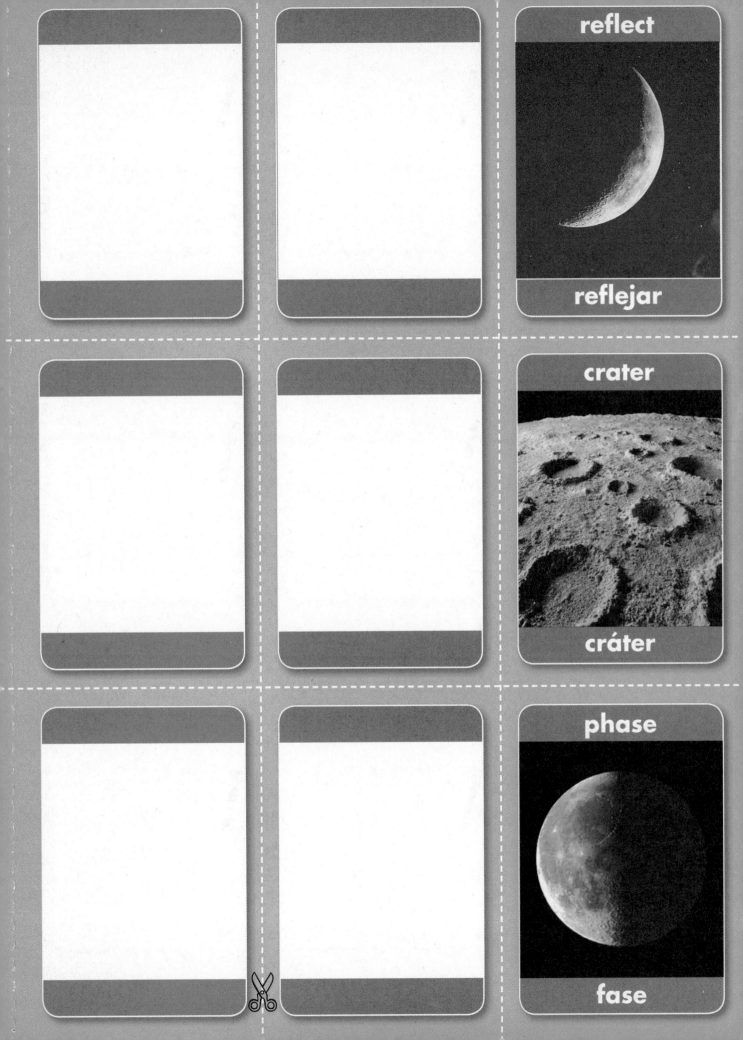

reflect

reflejar

crater

cráter

phase

fase

to bounce off

rebotar

a hole in the ground
shaped like a bowl

hueco con forma
de tazón que se
encuentra en la tierra

the shape of the
lighted part of
the moon

forma de la parte
iluminada de la Luna

REVIEW THE BIG ? How does weather change over time?

Lesson 1 What is weather?
- Weather is what the air outside is like.
- Moving air is called wind.

Lesson 2 How does weather change?
- Weather follows a pattern from day to day and from year to year.

Lesson 3 What are clouds?
- Water vapor changes into tiny drops of water or ice. These drops make different kinds of clouds.

Lesson 4 How can you stay safe in severe weather?
- You can make a plan to stay safe in severe weather.

Lesson 5 What does the sun do?
- The sun warms the water, land, and air.
- Shadows are made when light is blocked.

Lesson 6 How does the moon change?
- The moon moves in a path around Earth.
- The phases of the moon change.

Chapter Review

Lesson 1

2.2.1, 2.2.2, 2.NS.1, 2.NS.6

1. **Classify** (Circle) the tool that measures how much rain has fallen. **Write** how many centimeters of rain have fallen.

_____

2. **Describe Write** where air is.

_____

_____

_____

Lesson 2

2.2.4, 2.NS.4

◉ 3. **Compare and Contrast Write** how spring and fall are different.

_____

_____

_____

Lesson 3

2.2.3, 2.NS.1, 2.NS.4

4. **Predict Look** at the picture of the clouds. **Tell** what you think the weather will be like.

Lesson 4  2.2.6

5. Classify Draw a line from the picture to the word that goes with it.

(lightning)   (tornado)   (hurricane)

Lesson 5  2.2.5, 2.2.7, 2.NS.5, 2.NS.6, 2.NS.7

6. Evaluate Suppose your shadow looks very short. **Write** where you think the sun is in the sky.

_____

Lesson 6 ● 2.2.8, 2.2.9, 2.NS.1

7. Vocabulary Which sentence is not true about the moon? (Circle) the letter.

A. The moon reflects light.   C. The moon is round.

B. The moon makes its   D. It takes about a month to
   own light.   see all the moon's phases.

Got it?

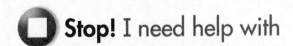

■ **Stop!** I need help with _____

▶ **Go!** Now I know _____

Does the sun warm land or water faster?

Materials

plastic cup with soil

plastic cup with water

2 thermometers

lamp

Inquiry Skill

Only one thing is changed in a **fair test.**

Ask a question.

Does sunlight warm soil or water faster?

Make a prediction.

1. Does soil or water warm faster in sunlight?

(a) soil

(b) water

Plan a fair test.

Use the same amount of soil and water.

Give both cups the same amount of light.

Design your test.

☑ **2.** Draw how you will set up your test.

  2.2.5 Ask questions and design class investigations on the effect of the sun heating the surface of the earth. **2.NS.4** Make predictions based on observations. **2.NS.6** Make and use simple equipment and tools to gather data and extend the senses. **2.NS.7** Recognize a fair test.

☑ **3.** List your steps.

_____

_____

_____

Do your test.

☑ **4.** Follow your steps.

Collect and record data.

☑ **5.** Fill in the chart.

Tell your conclusion.

6. Which warmed faster, the cup of soil or the cup of water?

_____

_____

7. Infer Do you think the sun warms land or water faster?

_____

_____

How to Stay Safe

Using Scientific Methods

1. Ask a question.
2. Make a hypothesis.
3. Plan a fair test.
4. Do your test.
5. Collect and record data.
6. Tell your conclusion.

Make a Poster

- Work with a partner.
- Make a poster about how to stay safe in thunderstorms, tornadoes, or hurricanes.
- Write a title at the top of the poster.
- Write words and draw pictures to show how to stay safe.
- Tell how to stay safe.
- Practice how to stay safe.

2.2.6

Make a Booklet

- Make a booklet about weather.
- Draw a picture of what the weather is like each day for a week.
- Show what you do and wear in different kinds of weather.

2.2.1

Phases of the Moon

- Use a calendar.
- Find out what the moon looks like every day for one month.

2.2.9

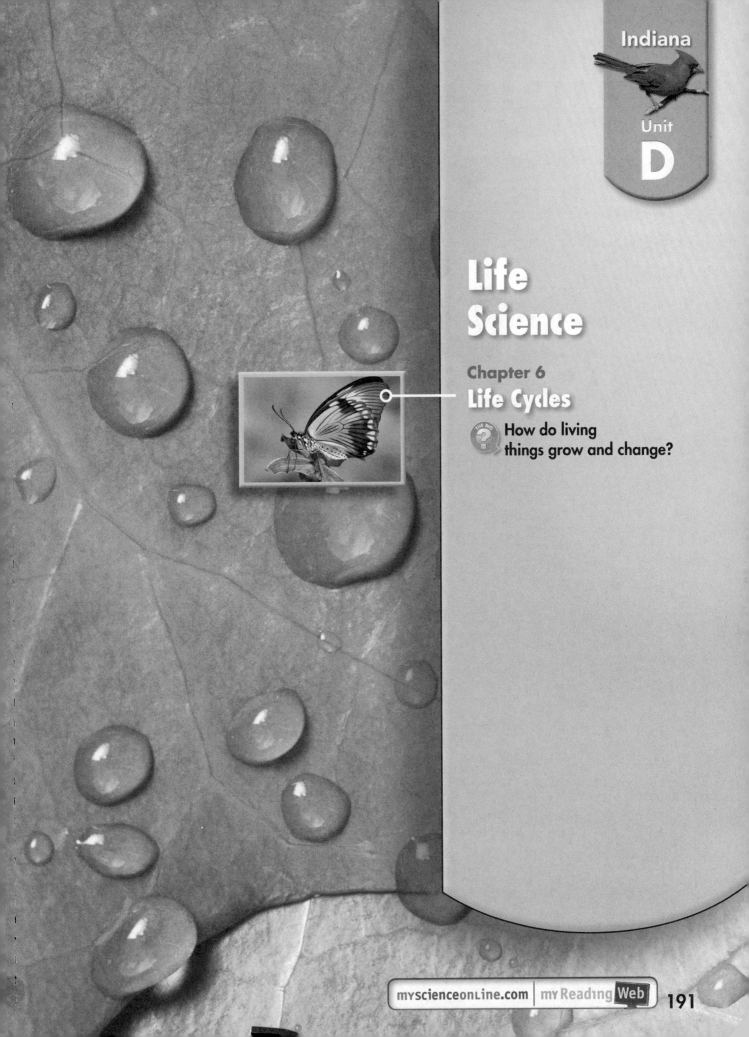

Life Science

Chapter 6

Life Cycles

How do living things grow and change?

What will it grow up to be?

Life Cycles

 Try It! How does a butterfly grow and change?

Lesson 1 What is the life cycle of a butterfly?
2.3.1, 2.3.2, 2.NS.3, 2.NS.4

Lesson 2 What is the life cycle of a frog?
2.3.1, 2.3.2, 2.NS.3, 2.NS.4

Lesson 3 What is the life cycle of a plant?
2.3.1, 2.3.2, 2.NS.2, 2.NS.3, 2.NS.7

Investigate It! What is the life cycle of a beetle?

Tell what you think the baby animal will grow up to be.

 How do living things grow and change?

Go to www.myscienceonline.com and click on: ⊗

 Untamed Science™
Watch the Ecogeeks in this wild video.

Got it? **60-Second Video**
Take one minute to learn science!

 **Science Songs**
Sing along with animated science songs!

Explore It! Animation
Quick and easy online experiments

How does a butterfly grow and change?

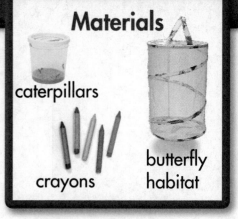

Materials

caterpillars

crayons

butterfly habitat

☑ 1. **Observe** the caterpillars every day for 3 weeks.

☑ 2. **Collect Data**   Write your observations.

Inquiry Skill When you **communicate**, you tell what you observe.

Week 1: _____

_____

Week 2: _____

_____

Week 3: _____

Explain Your Results

3. **Communicate**   Draw the stages you observed.

Butterfly Growth

   ➤   [ ]   ➤      ➤

2.3.1 Observing closely over a period of time, record in pictures and words the changes in plants and animals throughout their life cycles, including details of their body plan, structure and timing of growth, reproduction and death. **2.3.2** Compare and contrast details of body plan and structure within the life cycles of plants and animals. (Also **2.NS.3**)

⊙ **Sequence**

You put things in **sequence** when you tell what happens first, next, and last.

Life Cycle of a Chicken

First, an adult chicken lays an egg. Next, a chick hatches from the egg. The chick grows and changes. Last, the chick becomes an adult. The adult chicken may lay eggs.

Practice It!

Write which comes first, next, and last.

First **Next** **Last**

What is the life cycle of a butterfly?

2.3.1 Observing closely over a period of time, record in pictures and words the changes in plants and animals throughout their life cycles, including details of their body plan, structure and timing of growth, reproduction and death. 2.3.2 Compare and contrast details of body plan and structure within the life cycles of plants and animals. (Also 2.NS.3, 2.NS.4)

Envision It!

The young insect is changing.

my planet diary *for* **Indiana** **Did You Know?**

Read Together

Have you ever seen a tiger swallowtail butterfly? They can be found in Indiana. They live all over the eastern United States. They lay their eggs on the leaves of various trees, including the tulip tree. When the eggs hatch, the caterpillars eat the leaves.

Tiger swallowtail caterpillars have spots that look like eyes.

These butterflies are called swallowtails because their hind wings look as if they have tails. Their hind wings can look like the long pointed tails of swallows, a kind of bird.

Circle the part of the wings that look like tails.

Tiger swallowtail butterflies have yellow wings with black stripes.

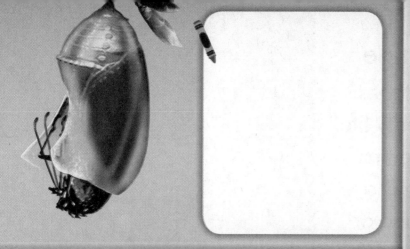

Draw what you think will come out.

Words to Know

life cycle

larva

pupa

Butterflies

Butterflies are insects. Insects have six legs. Look at the butterfly. First, it lands on a flower. Next, the butterfly drinks the nectar from the flower. The nectar is food for the butterfly. Last, the butterfly flies away.

Butterflies are living things. Living things grow and change. The way a living thing grows and changes is called its **life cycle.** Many young insects look very different when they become adult insects.

This butterfly gets what it needs from the flower.

⊙ **Sequence Write** what happens next and last.

First

A butterfly lands on a flower.

Next

Last

197

How Butterflies Change

Some insects have four stages in their life cycle. A butterfly life cycle has four stages. The first stage is the egg. The egg is a tiny object that has a round or oval shape.

The larva hatches from the egg after about four days. A **larva** is a young insect. The butterfly larva is called a caterpillar. The caterpillar is long, like a worm. Sometimes it has stripes or hairs. It eats a lot and grows very quickly. The caterpillar sheds its skin many times as it grows.

Draw what a caterpillar might look like when it first comes out of its egg.

These tiny eggs stick to the leaves.

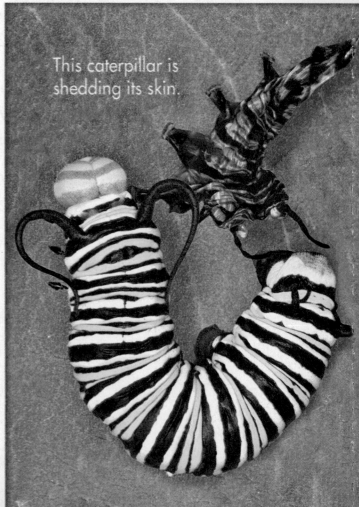
This caterpillar is shedding its skin.

This caterpillar has attached itself to a leaf. It is getting ready to become a pupa.

A chrysalis begins to form.

The caterpillar finds a place to attach itself after about two weeks. A hard covering called a chrysalis grows around the caterpillar. The caterpillar becomes a **pupa.** Wings begin to grow in the pupa stage.

Compare and **contrast** a butterfly larva and pupa. **Write** one way they are alike. **Write** one way they are different.

Butterfly Life Cycle

The adult butterfly breaks out of the chrysalis after about ten days. There is a complete change in the way it looks. It has wings and six legs.

Adult butterflies may fly long distances. They may lay eggs. The life cycle begins again.

Tell about the stages of the butterfly life cycle.

egg

caterpillar

Sequence Draw an ✗ on the stage after the larva stage.

butterfly

pupa

Lesson 2

What is the life cycle of a frog?

2.3.1 Observing closely over a period of time, record in pictures and words the changes in plants and animals throughout their life cycles, including details of their body plan, structure and timing of growth, reproduction and death. 2.3.2 Compare and contrast details of body plan and structure within the life cycles of plants and animals. (Also 2.NS.3, 2.NS.4)

Envision It!

Draw what you think is the correct order of stages in a frog's life cycle.

Inquiry **Explore It!**

How are life cycles alike and different?

☑ **1.** Put the Butterfly Life Cycle Cards in order. Glue the cards to the plates.

☑ **2.** Put the Frog Life Cycle Cards in order. Glue them to the other side of the plates.

Explain Your Results

3. Compare one stage of each life cycle.

_____

- -

_____

4. Communicate What changed during the frog's life cycle?

_____

_____

_____

Materials

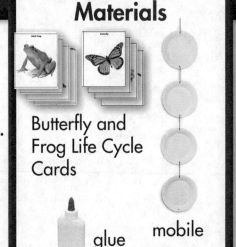

Butterfly and Frog Life Cycle Cards

glue   mobile

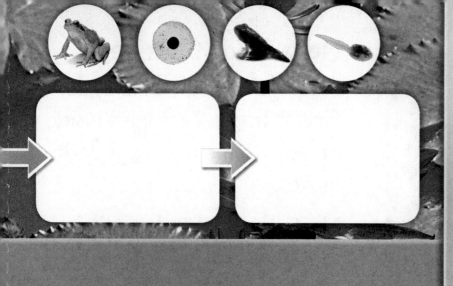

Word to Know

tadpole

Frogs

Frogs are amphibians. An amphibian is an animal that lives part of its life in the water. It lives part of its life on land too.

Very young frogs do not look like their parents. Young frogs go through many changes as they grow.

Underline two places that amphibians live.

Write about a place where a frog might live.

This frog uses its strong legs to escape its enemies.

Many tiny frog eggs are laid in the water. They feel like jelly.

Tadpoles begin life in water.

This tadpole is five weeks old. Its back legs have begun to grow.

How Frogs Change

Frogs go through a life cycle. First, a frog's life begins inside an egg. Some frog eggs float in water.

Next, the egg hatches. A tadpole swims out! A **tadpole** is a very young frog. The tadpole swims and breathes in the water. It has a tail and no legs. The tadpole grows and changes. The tadpole's back legs grow first. Later, the tadpole's front legs grow too.

Draw what a tadpole might look like when it is seven weeks old.

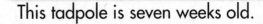

This tadpole is seven weeks old.

Then, it becomes a young frog. The young frog in the pictures is still growing. Its legs are getting stronger. Its tail is getting smaller.

Compare and **contrast** a tadpole that just hatched and a young frog. **Write** one way they are alike. **Write** one way they are different.

This tadpole is nine weeks old. Its front legs have begun to grow.

This young frog is twelve weeks old. It is becoming more like its parents.

Frog Life Cycle

The young frog grows and changes to become an adult frog. The adult frog can live on land or in the water. The frog hops on land. The adult frog does not have a tail. Frogs can live for many years.

An adult frog may lay eggs in the water. The life cycle begins again.

◉ **Sequence Draw** arrows to show the stages of the frog life cycle in order. **Tell** about the stages of the frog life cycle.

egg

adult frog

tadpole

young frog

Lightning Lab

How You Grow Older
Draw pictures of yourself. Put them in order. Begin with a baby picture. Glue them to a large piece of paper. Write down the changes you see.

What is the life cycle of a plant?

ⓘ 2.3.1 Observing closely over a period of time, record in pictures and words the changes in plants and animals throughout their life cycles, including details of their body plan, structure and timing of growth, reproduction and death. 2.3.2 Compare and contrast details of body plan and structure within the life cycles of plants and animals. (Also 2.NS.2, 2.NS.3, 2.NS.7)

Envision It!

Draw what you think the acorn will look like when it is grown.

Inquiry **Explore It!**

How does a seed grow?

☐ **1.** Put the seeds on the paper towel. Put the towel in the bag.

☐ **2.** Seal the bag. Put it in a warm place.

☐ **3.** **Observe** the seeds every other day. **Record** your observations.

Materials

6 pinto bean seeds

wet paper towel

resealable plastic bag

hand lens

Observations	
Day 1	
Day 3	
Day 5	
Day 7	
Day 9	

Explain Your Results

4. Which parts grew first? **Predict** what will happen next.

_____

_____

ⓘ **2.NS.2** Conduct investigations that may happen over time as a class, in small groups, or independently. **2.NS.4** Make predictions based on observations.

Words to Know

pollen
seedling

Flowers

Many plants have flowers. A flower makes seeds. Look at the flower on this page. The outside part of the flower is called a petal. Petals are often colored. Colorful petals may attract bees and other insects.

A powder called pollen is found inside the flower. **Pollen** is needed to make seeds grow.

Tell why you think colorful petals can help make seeds.

Wind and insects move pollen to this part of the flower. Seeds begin to grow.

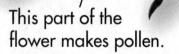

This part of the flower makes pollen.

Fruits

Many plants grow from seeds. Fruit forms around the seeds as they grow. Fruits cover and protect seeds. The seeds might make new plants. You can see the seeds inside apples and ears of corn.

The seeds can be spread in many different ways. Some seeds are spread by air or water. Some seeds are spread by animals. People can spread the seeds too. New plants might begin to grow if they get the water, air, and space they need.

Underline one reason fruits are important.

Seeds are inside each apple. The fruit of the apple protects the seeds.

Burs are fruits that can travel by hooking onto something.

Each kernel of corn is a fruit.

Seeds

A seed has a hard covering called a seed coat. The seed coat protects the seed. Each seed has material that will become a plant. Food is stored around the new plant. The plant uses the stored food as it grows.

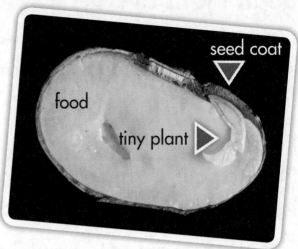

food

tiny plant

seed coat

Compare the tiny bean plant above and the bean plants below.
Write one way they are alike.
Write one way they are different.

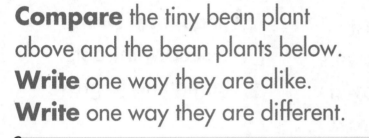

Bean Plant Life Cycle

First, a bean plant is a seed. A seed that gets enough water and air might begin to grow.

Roots grow down into the ground. Next, a young plant grows out of the ground. It is called a **seedling.**

The plant continues to grow. Last, the plant becomes an adult. Flowers grow on the adult plant. The flowers make seeds. Some seeds will grow into new plants. The life cycle begins again.

Sequence Draw a seed with roots beginning to grow.

Go Green

Air in Soil

Roots cannot get air when soil is packed too hard. Plant a seed in a cup of loose soil. Plant a seed in a cup of packed soil. Water both and observe. Put your healthy plant in the ground. It will help clean the air.

seed

Tell about the stages in the life cycle of a bean plant.

Flowers grow on the adult bean plant.

seedling

What is the life cycle of a beetle?

Follow a Procedure

☐ **1. Observe** the mealworms.

Be careful! They are alive! Handle with care.

Inquiry Skill
You **record data** when you draw what you observe.

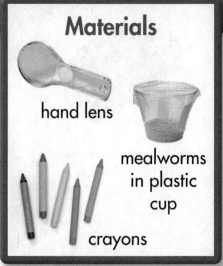

☐ **2. Collect Data** Draw 2 stages you see.

2.3.1 Observing closely over a period of time, record in pictures and words the changes in plants and animals throughout their life cycles, including details of their body plan, structure and timing of growth, reproduction and death. **2.3.2** Compare and contrast details of body plan and structure within the life cycles of plants and animals. (Also **2.NS.3**)

3. Observe the mealworms for 3 weeks. Look for a new stage.

4. Draw the 3 stages.

Analyze and Conclude

5. **UNLOCK THE BIG ?** **Interpret Data** How did the mealworm change?

_____

_____

_____

6. Infer How is a beetle pupa like a butterfly pupa?

_____

_____

_____

Compare Size and Age

Do the math!

6 years old

10 years old

2 years old

As people grow, their size changes. The girl in this picture has grown. The table shows how tall the girl was as she grew.

Age	Size
2 years old	36 inches tall
6 years old	49 inches tall
10 years old	61 inches tall

Write how many inches the girl grew from when she was six years old to when she was ten years old. Use the number sentence to help you find the answer.

61 in. - 49 in. = _____

Tell how many inches the girl grew from when she was two years old to when she was ten years old.

Vocabulary Smart Cards

life cycle
larva
pupa
tadpole
pollen
seedling

Play a Game!

Cut out the cards.

Work with a partner.

One person puts the cards picture side up.

The other person puts the cards picture side down.

Work together to match each word with its meaning.

217

tadpole

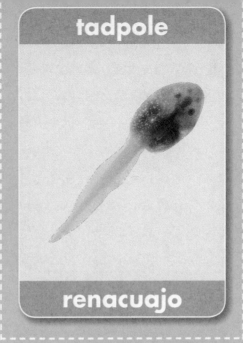

renacuajo

life cycle

ciclo de vida

pollen

polen

larva

larva

seedling

plántula

pupa

pupa

the way a living thing
grows and changes

manera en que un ser
vivo crece y cambia

a very young frog

una rana muy joven

a young insect

un insecto joven

a powder that can
make seeds grow

polvo que puede
hacer que las semillas
crezcan

stage in an insect's
life between larva
and adult

etapa de la vida de
un insecto entre larva
y adulto

a young plant

una planta joven

218

Lesson 1

What is the life cycle of a butterfly?

- A butterfly's life cycle includes an egg, a larva, a pupa, and an adult.

Lesson 2

What is the life cycle of a frog?

- A frog's life cycle includes an egg, a tadpole, a young frog, and an adult frog.

Lesson 3

What is the life cycle of a plant?

- A bean plant's life cycle includes a seed, a seedling, and an adult plant.

Lesson 1 2.3.1, 2.3.2, 2.NS.3, 2.NS.4

1. Vocabulary Complete the sentence. The way a living thing grows and changes is called its _____.

2. Analyze Write how a larva is different from a butterfly.

_____
_____
_____
_____

Lesson 2 2.3.1, 2.3.2, 2.NS.3, 2.NS.4

3. Vocabulary Draw a line from the picture to the word that goes with it.

egg   frog   tadpole

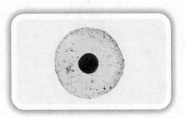

4. Compare Write how the life cycle of a frog is like the life cycle of a butterfly.

_____
_____

Lesson 3 🟠 2.3.1, 2.3.2, 2.NS.2, 2.NS.3, 2.NS.7

5. Describe Write two ways that seeds can be spread.

_____

_____

_____

◉**6. Sequence** What is the second stage in the life cycle of a bean plant? (Circle) the letter.

A. seed   C. seedling

B. adult   D. seed coat

Got it?

☐ **Stop!** I need help with _____

_____

_____

▶ **Go!** Now I know _____

_____

_____

Does a radish grow more with or without light?

Materials

6 radish seeds

soil

2 paper cups

water

ruler

Inquiry Skill
Plan an **experiment** to test your prediction.

Ask a question.

Does a radish grow more with or without light?

Make a prediction.

1. A plant will grow better if it gets

a) a full day of light.
b) two hours of light.

 **Be careful!** Do not put any materials in your mouth.

Plan a fair test.

Make sure you use the same setup for both cups.

Design your test.

☑ **2.** List your steps.

_____

_____

_____

_____

_____

_____

2.3.1 Observing closely over a period of time, record in pictures and words the changes in plants and animals throughout their life cycles, including details of their body plan, structure and timing of growth, reproduction and death. **2.3.2** Compare and contrast details of body plan and structure within the life cycles of plants and animals. **2.NS.4** Make predictions based on observations. **2.NS.7** Recognize a fair test. (Also **2.NS.2**)

_____

Do your test.

☑ **3.** Follow your steps.

Collect and record data.

☑ **4.** Fill in the chart.

Record your measurements.

Tell your conclusion.

5. Communicate   Which grew more?

_____

_____

_____

Make a Puzzle

- Draw a picture of a butterfly life cycle on heavy paper.

- Label each stage in your picture.

- Cut your picture into pieces to make a puzzle.

- Give your puzzle to a partner to put together.

- Tell your partner about your picture.

🔵 2.3.1, 2.3.2

Put On a Play

- Pretend to be an animal or plant.

- Act out what your animal or plant does.

- Show other things about your animal or plant.

- See if your classmates can guess what you are.

🔵 2.3.1, 2.3.2

Temperature and Seeds

- Gather some seeds.

- Find out if seeds will grow faster in a cold place or in a warm place.

🔵 2.3.1, 2.NS.2, 2.NS.3, 2.NS.7

Using Scientific Methods

1. Ask a question.

2. Make a hypothesis.

3. Plan a fair test.

4. Do your test.

5. Collect and record data.

6. Tell your conclusion.

Metric and Customary Measurements

Science uses the metric system to measure things.
Metric measurement is used around the world.
Here is how different metric measurements
compare to customary measurements.

1 liter

1 cup

Fahrenheit

Celsius

°F °C

Temperature
Water freezes at 0°C, or 32°F.
Water boils at 100°C, or 212°F.

Volume
One liter is greater
than 4 cups.

1 kilogram

1 pound

Mass
One kilogram is greater
than 2 pounds.

1 meter

1 foot

Length and Distance
One meter is longer than 3 feet.

Glossary

The glossary uses letters and signs to show how words are pronounced. The mark ′ is placed after a syllable with a primary or heavy accent. The mark ′ is placed after a syllable with a secondary or lighter accent.

To hear these vocabulary words and definitions, you can refer to the AudioText CD, or log on to the digital path's Vocabulary Smart Cards.

Pronunciation Key

a in hat	ō in open	sh in she
ā in age	ȯ in all	th in thin
â in care	ô in order	ŦH in then
ä in far	oi in oil	zh in measure
e in let	ou in out	ə = a in about
ē in equal	u in cup	ə = e in taken
ėr in term	u̇ in put	ə = i in pencil
i in it	ü in rule	ə = o in lemon
ī in ice	ch in child	ə = u in circus
o in hot	ng in long	

A

attract (ə trakt′) To pull toward. The opposite poles of two magnets will **attract** one another.

atraer Jalar hacia sí. Los polos opuestos de un imán **se atraen** uno al otro.

conclusion (kən klü′ zhən) What you decide after you think about all you know. Scientists repeat their tests before drawing a **conclusion.**

conclusión Lo que decides después de pensar en lo que sabes. Los científicos repiten sus pruebas antes de sacar una **conclusión.**

crater (krā′ tər) A hole in the ground shaped like a bowl. There are many **craters** on the surface of the moon.

cráter Hueco con forma de tazón que se encuentra en la tierra. Hay muchos **cráteres** en la superficie de la Luna.

data (dā′ tə) What you observe. Scientists collect **data** while working.

datos Lo que observas. Los científicos reúnen **datos** cuando trabajan.

dissolve (di zolv′) To spread throughout a liquid. Sugar **dissolves** in lemonade.

disolver Combinar una o más sustancias en un líquido. El azúcar **se disuelve** en la limonada.

evaporate (i vap′ ə rāt) To change from a liquid to a gas. Water **evaporates** when it changes into water vapor.

evaporarse Cambiar de líquido a gas. El agua se **se evapora** cuando se convierte en vapor de agua.

F

force (fôrs) A push or pull that makes something move. The man uses **force** to throw the ball.

fuerza Empujón o jalón que hace que algo se mueva. El hombre usa la **fuerza** para lanzar la pelota.

G

gas (gas) Matter that does not have its own size or shape. Bubbles are filled with **gas.**

gas Materia que no tiene tamaño o forma propios. Las burbujas están llenas de **gas.**

goal (gōl) Something you want to do. People set a **goal** to find a solution.

objetivo Algo que quieres hacer. Escogemos un **objetivo** para encontrar una solución.

gravity (grav′ ə tē) A force that pulls things toward the center of Earth. **Gravity** is pulling the toy down.

gravedad Fuerza que jala los objetos hacia el centro de la Tierra. La **gravedad** jala el juguete hacia abajo.

H

hypothesis (hī poth′ ə sis) A possible answer to a question. Scientists decide if a **hypothesis** is supported or not supported.

hipótesis Respuesta posible a una pregunta. Los científicos deciden si una **hipótesis** tiene bases firmes o no.

I

inquiry (in kwī′ rē) Asking questions and looking for answers. Scientists use **inquiry** to learn.

indagación Hacer preguntas y buscar respuestas. Los científicos hacen **indagaciones** para aprender.

invent (in vent′) To make something for the first time. Scientists **invented** cars that use both gasoline and electricity.

inventar Hacer algo por primera vez. Los científicos **inventaron** carros que usan tanto gasolina como electricidad.

L

larva (lär′ və) A young insect. A butterfly **larva** is called a caterpillar.

larva Un insecto joven. La **larva** de una mariposa se llama oruga.

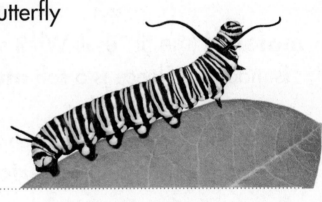

life cycle (līf sī′ kəl) The way a living thing grows and changes. We studied the **life cycle** of a butterfly.

ciclo de vida Manera en que un ser vivo crece y cambia. Hoy estudiamos el **ciclo de vida** de la mariposa.

liquid (lik′ wid) Matter that has its own volume but takes the shape of its container. The **liquid** changes shape in the tubes.

líquido Materia que tiene su propio volumen pero que toma la forma del recipiente que la contiene. El **líquido** cambia de forma dentro de los tubos.

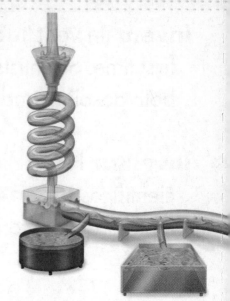

M

material (mə tir′ ē əl) What something is made of. Fleece is a soft **material.**

material De lo que está hecho algo. El tejido polar es un **material** suave.

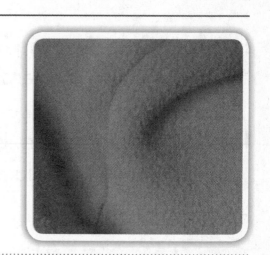

matter (mat′ ər) Anything that takes up space and has mass. Everything is made of **matter.**

materia Todo lo que ocupa espacio y tiene masa. Todo está hecho de **materia.**

mixture (miks′ chər) Something made up of two or more kinds of matter. This fruit salad is a **mixture** of different fruits.

mezcla Algo formado por varios tipos de materia. Esta ensalada es una **mezcla** de frutas.

motion (mō′ shən) The act of moving. A merry-go-round moves in a circular **motion.**

movimiento El acto de moverse. Los carruseles siguen un **movimiento** circular.

observe (əb sėrv′) To use your senses to find out about something. You can **observe** how an apple looks, sounds, feels, smells, and tastes.

observar Usar tus sentidos para descubrir algo. Puedes **observar** el aspecto de una manzana, cómo suena, cómo es cuando la tocas, a qué huele y a qué sabe.

pattern (pat′ ərn) The way something repeats itself. Weather follows a **pattern.**

patrón La manera en que algo se repite. El tiempo sigue un **patrón.**

phase (fāz) The shape of the lighted part of the moon. The moon's **phases** can be seen best at night.

fase Forma de la parte iluminada de la Luna. Las **fases** de la Luna se ven mejor de noche.

pollen (pol′ ən) A powder that can make seeds grow. Wind and insects can move **pollen** from flower to flower.

polen Polvo que puede hacer que las semillas crezcan. El viento y los insectos pueden transportar el **polen** de flor en flor.

position (pə zish′ ən) Where an object is. You can describe the girl's **position.**

posición Donde está un objeto. Puedes describir la **posición** de la niña.

precipitation (pri sip′ ə tā′ shən) The water that falls to Earth. Snow is a kind of **precipitation.**

precipitación El agua que cae a la Tierra. La nieve es un tipo de **precipitación.**

property (prop′ ər tē) Something about an object that you can observe with your senses. An object's color is one kind of **property.**

propiedad Algo en un objeto que puedes observar con tus sentidos. El color de un objeto es una **propiedad** de ese objeto.

pupa (pyü′ pə) Stage in an insect's life between larva and adult. When a caterpillar is changing inside its covering, it is called a **pupa.**

pupa Etapa en la vida de un insecto entre larva y adulto. Cuando la oruga cambia dentro de la cubierta que la protege, se llama **pupa.**

R

reflect (ri flekt′) To bounce off. The moon **reflects** the sun's light.

reflejar Rebotar. La luz del Sol se **refleja** en la Luna.

repel (ri pel′) To push away. The north ends of magnets will **repel** each other.

repeler Apartar algo empujándolo. Los polos norte de dos imanes **se repelen** uno al otro.

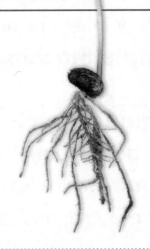

seedling (sēd′ ling) A young plant. The tree **seedling** grows into a tree.

plántula Una planta joven. La **plántula** crece y se convierte en un árbol.

severe weather (sə vēr′ weŦH′ ər) Dangerous weather. It is important to be ready for **severe weather.**

tiempo severo Tiempo peligroso. Es importante estar preparado para el **tiempo severo.**

shadow (shad′ ō) The shape that is made when an object blocks the light. **Shadows** are long in the evening.

sombra Forma que se ve cuando un objeto bloquea la luz. Las **sombras** son largas por la tarde.

simple machine (sim′ pəl mə shēn′)
Tool with few or no moving parts. A
simple machine can make work easier.

máquina simple Instrumento sin, o
con pocas, partes que se mueven. Una
máquina simple puede hacer que el
trabajo sea más fácil.

solid (sol′ id) Matter that keeps its
own size and shape. The case that
holds the supplies is a **solid.**

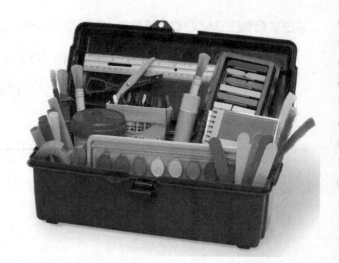

sólido Materia que mantiene
tamaño y forma propios. La caja
de útiles de pintura es un **sólido.**

T

tadpole (tad′ pōl) A very young frog. Rosie
caught **tadpoles** in a pond.

renacuajo Una rana muy joven. Rosie atrapó
un **renacuajo** en el estanque.

technology (tek nol/ ə jē) The use of science to solve problems. People use **technology** every day.

tecnología El uso de la ciencia para resolver problemas. Usamos la **tecnología** todos los días.

thermometer (thər mom/ ə tər) A tool that measures temperature. You can use a **thermometer** to measure how hot or cold something is.

termómetro Instrumento para medir la temperatura. Puedes usar un **termómetro** para medir cuán caliente o cuán frío está algo.

tool (tül) Something that is used to do work. Some **tools** are used to observe.

instrumento Algo que se usa para hacer trabajo. Algunos **instrumentos** se usan para observar.

volume (vol⁄ yəm) The amount of space matter takes up. You can use a measuring cup to measure the **volume** of liquids.

volumen Cantidad de espacio que ocupa la materia. Puedes usar una taza de medir para medir el **volumen** de un líquido.

water vapor (wȯ′ tər vā′ pər) A form of water in the air. You cannot see **water vapor.**

vapor de agua Una forma del agua en el aire. El **vapor de agua** no se puede ver.

wind (wind) Moving air. **Wind** can be very powerful.

viento Aire que se mueve. El **viento** puede ser muy fuerte.

Index

This index lists the pages on which topics appear in this book. Page numbers after a *p* refer to a photograph. Page numbers following a *c* refer to a chart or graph.

Credits

Staff Credits

The people who made up the *Interactive Science* team — representing composition services, core design digital and multimedia production services, digital product development, editorial, editorial services, manufacturing, and production — are listed below.

Geri Amani, Alisa Anderson, Jose Arrendondo, Amy Austin, Scott Baker, Lindsay Bellino, Charlie Bink, Bridget Binstock, Holly Blessen, Robin Bobo, Craig Bottomley, Jim Brady, Laura Brancky, Chris Budzisz, Mary Chingwa, Sitha Chhor, Caroline Chung, Margaret Clampitt, Kier Cline, Brandon Cole, Mitch Coulter, AnnMarie Coyne, Fran Curran, Dana Damiano, Nancy Duffner, Amanda Ferguson, David Gall, Mark Geyer, Amy Goodwin, Gerardine Griffin, Chris Haggerty, Laura Hancko, Jericho Hernandez, Autumn Hickenlooper, Guy Huff, George Jacobson, Marian Jones, Kathi Kalina, Chris Kammer, Sheila Kanitsch, Alyse Kondrat, Mary Kramer, Thea Limpus, Dominique Mariano, Lori McGuire, Melinda Medina, Angelina Mendez, Claudi Mimo, John Moore, Phoebe Novak, Anthony Nuccio, Jeffrey Osier, Julianne Regnier, Charlene Rimsa, Rebecca Roberts, Camille Salerno, Manuel Sanchez, Carol Schmitz, Amanda Seldera, Sheetal Shah, Jeannine Shelton El, Geri Shulman, Greg Sorenson, Samantha Sparkman, Mindy Spelius, Karen Stockwell, Dee Sunday, Dennis Tarwood, Jennie Teece, Lois Teesdale, Michaela Tudela, Oscar Vera, Dave Wade, Tom Wickland, James Yagelski, Tim Yetzina, Diane Zimmermann.

Illustrations

78, 97, 162, 163, 190, 211, 213 Precision Graphics
All other illustrations Chandler Digital Art

Photographs

Every effort has been made to secure permission and provide appropriate credit for photographic material. The publisher deeply regrets any omission and pledges to correct errors called to its attention in subsequent editions.

Unless otherwise acknowledged, all photographs are the property of Pearson Education, Inc.

Photo locators denoted as follows: Top (T), Center (C), Bottom (B), Left (L), Right (R), Background (Bkgd)

COVER: ©Eric Isselée/Shutterstock

1 (TC) ©Bernd Mellmann/Alamy Images, (TC) ©Panoramic Images/Getty Images, (BC) ©Richard Orton/Jupiter Images, (BC) ©Vladimir Daragan/Shutterstock; 2 ©Purestock/Getty Images; 6 (B) JSC/NASA; 7 (CR) ©Hemis/Alamy Images; 8 ©Michael Rosenfeld/Getty Images; 9 (R) ©AFP/Getty Images, (L) ©Jeff Greenberg/PhotoEdit, Inc.; 10 (TR) ©Panoramic Images/Getty Images; 11 (CR) ©Peter Dazeley/Getty Images; 12 ©Photononstop/SuperStock; 14 (TR) ©Getty Images/Jupiter Images; 15 (CR) Mary Clark; 19 ©Anderson Ross/Getty Images; 20 (TR) ©Gordon Wiltsie/Getty Images; 21 (CR) ©Getty Images/Jupiter Images; 24 (TR) ©Andreas Scheler/Alamy; 25 (CR) James Osmond/Alamy Images; 26 (T) Colin Keates/Courtesy of the Natural History Museum, London/©DK Images, (C) DK Images; 30 (C) ©Jet Propulsion Laboratry/NASA Image Exchange, (TR) NASA; 31 (TL) ©Getty Images/Jupiter Images, (TR) ©Hemis/Alamy Images, (CR) ©Photononstop/SuperStock, (BL) James Osmond/Alamy Images, (BR) Mary Clark; 33 (BL) ©Andreas Scheler/Alamy, (BC) ©Gordon Wiltsie/Getty Images, (T) ©Michael Rosenfeld/Getty Images, (TC) ©Photononstop/SuperStock, (B) ©Purestock/Getty Images, (C) Mary Clark; 34 (B) Jupiter Images; 35 ©Nigel Cattlin/Alamy Images; 36 ©Jim Esposito Photography L. L. C./Getty Images; 39 (T) ©Gayane/Shutterstock, (C) ©Nando/Shutterstock; 40 (B) ©Bernd Mellmann/Alamy Images, (TR) Getty Images; 41 (BR) ©Reuters/Corbis; 42 (BCR) ©JG Photography/Alamy, (BL) Dave King/Courtesy of The Science Museum, London/©DK Images, (CL) DK Images, (BCL) Simon Clay/Courtesy of the National Motor Museum, Beaulieu/©DK Images; 43 (BC) ©DK Images, (TR) ©Paul Maguire/Shutterstock, (BR) ©Roy Stevens/Time & Life Pictures/Getty Images, (BL) Image Courtesy Eastman Kodak Company; 44 (TR) ©Mike Flippo/Shutterstock; 45 (CR) ©Peter Gridley/Getty Images; 46 (TR) ©Paul Tearle/Thinkstock; 47 (CR) ©Denis and Yulia Pogostins/Shutterstock; 48 (Bkgd) ©Evgeny Murtola/Shutterstock; 49 (B) ©Blend Images/SuperStock; 50 (TR) ©Emmanuel Lattes/Alamy Images; 51 (CR) ©Comstock/Thinkstock, (B) Photos to Go/Photolibrary; 52 (TC) ©Massimiliano Leban/iStockphoto, (TR) ©SuperStock RF/SuperStock; 53 (CL) ©Andre Baranowski/Getty Images, (TL) ©Comstock/Thinkstock, (CR) ©David Madison/Getty Images, (TR) ©Losevsky Pavel/Shutterstock, (BR) ©Mike Kemp/Getty Images; 54 (BR) ©Frank Cezus/Getty Images, (BL) ©Jason Kasumovic/Shutterstock, (C) ©PhotoObjects/Thinkstock, (BBL) Clive Streeter/©DK Images; 55 (C) ©Brand X Pictures/Thinkstock, (BR) ©John E. Marriot/Getty Images, (BL) ©Mitsuaki Iwago/Minden Pictures, (CR) Peter Anderson/©DK Images; 58 Matt Cashore Photography/From the Collection of Studebaker National Museum, South Bend, Indiana; 59 (CL) ©Comstock/Thinkstock, (BR) ©Peter Gridley/Getty Images, (CR) ©Reuters/Corbis, (TR) Getty Images; 61 (CL) ©Blend Images/SuperStock, (BL) ©Brand X Pictures/Thinkstock, (B) ©Jim Esposito Photography L. L. C./Getty Images, (TL) Getty Images; 63 (TC) ©Massimiliano Leban/iStockphoto, (TR) Photos to Go/Photolibrary; 64 ©Margaret Durrance/Photo Researchers, Inc.; 67 (T) ©age fotostock/SuperStock; 68 (B) ©Kevin Fleming/Corbis; 69 (CR) ©Kim Karpeles/Alamy Images; 75 (BR, BL) Digital Vision; 80 (BL) ©3C Stock/Alamy Images, (C) ©David Trood/Getty Images; 82 (TR) Jupiter Images; 84 (TC) ©Craig Tuttle/Corbis; 85 (Bkgd) ©Derrick Alderman/Alamy Images; 86 (BC) ©Art & Vision/Alamy Images, (BL) ©Image Source , (BL) ©Philip and Karen Smith/Getty Images, (Bkgd) ©Vladimir Daragan/Shutterstock; 87 (TR) ©Viktor1/Shutterstock, (CR) Gary Ombler/©DK Images; 88 (TR) ©Masterfile Royalty-Free; 90 ©Blend Images/SuperStock; 91 (TR) ©Getty Images/Thinkstock; 92 (Bkgd) ©Emrah Turudu/Getty Images; 97 (BL) ©David Trood/Getty Images, (TR) ©Kim Karpeles/Alamy Images; 99 (TC) ©Blend Images/SuperStock; 101 (B) ©Margaret Durrance/Photo Researchers, Inc., (BC) Jupiter Images; 102 (CR, C) Dave king/©DK Images, (BL) Getty

Take Note

This space is yours. Draw pictures and write words.

This is your book.

You can write in it.

This is your book.

You can write in it.